You don't have to go it alone

Leslie B. Flynn

ACCENT BOOKS

Denver, Colorado

ACCENT BOOKS
A division of Accent Publications, Inc.
12100 W. Sixth Avenue
P.O. Box 15337
Denver, Colorado 80215

Library of Congress Catalog Card Number: 80-66722
ISBN 0-89636-058X

882-1109

Dedication

This book is dedicated to the members of my congregation among whom for over three decades I have witnessed countless incidents of caring for one another.

CONTENTS

FOREWORD

A Christian living alone in a large city lamented that, if she died after work on Friday, the first to miss her would probably be her fellow-workers on Monday morning, not her fellow-believers on Sunday morning.

In this day of high mobility and increasing depersonalization many Christians seem to have few or no friends. One of the most important ministries a believer may exercise is reaching out genuinely to other believers who seem to be loners.

Experts in the field of interpersonal effectiveness tell us that a person, to stay psychologically healthy, has to have good relationships with other individuals. Not strange, then, that the New Testament teaches that a believer's spiritual health requires good relationships with fellow-believers. We cannot go it alone. This is why the New Testament has so many commands involving "one another".

For years evangelical churches have stressed the three "b's"; the *blood,* the *Bible* and the *blessed hope.* Recently a fourth emphasis has been added—*brother.* It is hoped that this meditation will help each of us to become a better brother to another.

In a cruel world, and in often an unfriendly church, we sorely need to practice New Testament *one-another-manship.*

Everybody needs somebody.

1
We Need Each Other

A seminary professor asked one of his students to occupy his house during vacation as protection against burglars. Aroused in the middle of the night by a strange sound, the student groggily groped for his glasses.

He had gone to sleep with one arm in an awkward position, cutting off circulation to that limb. As he reached for the dresser, he encountered his own now cold and clammy hand. With a shudder he jumped to a standing position and shouted to his wife, "There's a hand under the bed!"

She bolted out of bed and began feeling along the wall for the light switch. Suddenly a thought came to him: "Why am I using only one hand?" Even before his wife found the switch, the embarrassing truth dawned on him. The hand was his own.

The student never forgot the incident. In striking fashion he learned that when one member of the body

9

loses contact with another member, mischief may result. How like the body of Christ! Believers belong to each other. We need each other.

MAN NOT MEANT TO BE ALONE

The divine dictum, "It is not good for man to be alone," extends far beyond the need for a marriage mate. People seek community one way or another, perhaps in clubs or organizations like the Rotary, Kiwanis, Lions or American Legion, or in the various lodges. Then there are Country Clubs. Rock concerts, centering around music and marijuana, provide camaraderie for millions of youth. The cocktail party is one popular version of "fellowship." In this contrived atmosphere a communal feeling of well-being loosens clammed-up tongues to tell secrets generally not repeated, and encourages understanding from others similarly stupored.

A prisoner for years in North Vietnam, Howard Rutledge claims in his book, *In the Presence of Mine Enemies,* that no torture is worse than years of solitary confinement. He relates the need for communication was so great, U.S. POWs in the Hanoi Hilton soon set up a system of covert conversation techniques—tapping, coded notes, coughs, sliding sandals—by which to talk to each other every day, sharing private details about each other's family life, military career and religious faith. Though walls separated, they learned how important each was to the other.[1]

Even people who move freely among others may be desperately alone. The Department of Psychiatry of Harvard Medical School studied in depth the lives of six middle-class couples who had moved across at least two state lines in order for the husband to work in the Boston area.

Having much in common with their new business colleagues, the husbands were not upset by their new locale. However, soon after the move, four of the six wives were seriously unhappy and complained of isolation.

The two who were not seriously unhappy made determined efforts to break out of their isolation; one by taking a job, the other by spending several days getting acquainted in her new neighborhood. The study concluded that people do indeed have needs that can be met only through interpersonal relationships. All of us have a need to know people who share our concerns and on whom we can depend in a pinch.

"Lonely Voices" is not just the title of a song. Some counselors contend that loneliness is the most widespread illness in America today, and have given it the technical term, *meaningless depersonalization.* Many who are not isolated in space are insulated in spirit.

A man riding in a cab in Times Square was handed this note, "I'd rather you talk to me than tip me. I'm lonely. Your driver."

A lady remarked that if she heard of just one more anonymous organization she would scream. She knew of Alcoholics Anonymous, Gamblers Anonymous, Migraines Anonymous, Dropouts Anonymous, Asthmatics Anonymous, Overeaters Anonymous, and Parents of Youth in Trouble Anonymous.

A wise, disagreeing person pointed out that the emphasis is not on anonymity, but on the problem which unifies those who suffer from it. Also, the cloak of anonymity protects people from whatever shame or stigma may be placed on them by an unsympathetic public. How wonderful to be able to verbalize your problem in the presence of another struggling with the same situation.

11

You Don't Have to Go It Alone

Moreover, the emotional support of those who have conquered can be so fortifying. It may be true that misery loves company, but it is also true that company can reduce misery. A visitor at an Alcoholics Anonymous meeting noticed with what feeling they prayed together, "Forgive *us* our trespasses. Deliver *us* from evil."

In a clever takeoff on John Donne's famous words, "No man is an island," Trans-Canada Telephone System ran an ad with the heading, "No branch is an island." Says the ad, "Isolation is destructive." Communication with other branches of the human tree is essential for a person's healthy growth.

Someone said, "Whoever is delighted in solitude is either a wild beast or a god." This proverb is inaccurate, however, for God is not a secluded but a social Being, a togetherness Deity. The members of the Trinity have each other to love and communicate with—Father with Son, Son with Spirit, and Spirit with Father. And God, creating man in His divine image, made him a social, relational creature. Man was not meant to be alone, but to have communion on a meaningful level with his fellowmen. As someone put it, we need "some sun, some fun, and some one."

THE CHURCH PROVIDES FELLOWSHIP

Believers in Christ are joined in the closest possible relationship—the family of God. The Apostles' Creed calls it the "communion of saints." Paul spoke of the church as the body, with Christ as Head and believers as members, each functioning smoothly for the health of the whole.

Because of this oneness, Christians gravitate toward each other. On a voyage back to Jerusalem, Paul and his companions found disciples at Tyre when the boat stopped to unload cargo (Acts 21:3,4). The *Pulpit Commentary* suggests that the apostolic band had to seek out believers scattered throughout the city and perhaps found them with difficulty. But Christian fellowship was important to them.

Fellowship is an interesting word, both in English and in Greek. In English it comes from the Anglo-Saxon fee-lowship. *Fee* means *cow*, the form wealth took in those days. Neighbors put their cows together, breaking down the fence between them to show trust in each other, creating fee-lowship through their joint cow-account. This reminds us of early believers who, continuing steadfast in fellowship, gave lands and houses to help those in need (Acts 2:42,45).

The Greek word for fellowship is *koinonia*, coming from *koinos*, meaning common. The noun *koinonos* means partner. Fellowship is to have in common with a partner. Two sets of brothers, James and John, and Peter and Andrew, partners in fishing later became partners in fishing for men (Luke 5:10; John 1:40). Paul thanked the Philippians for their partnership in the gospel, referring probably to their financial contribution which helped Paul spread the truth (Philippians 1:5).

When James, Peter and John gave the right hand of fellowship to Paul and Barnabas, it was not a sign of reconciliation for there had never been strife, but it was a mark of partnership in the common undertaking of proclaiming the gospel, one group going to the Jews and the other to the Gentiles (Galatians 2:9).

Bible scholars suggest that two is the perfect number for witnessing because the second confirms the word of the first. The two Testaments, Old and New, give witness to man of God's revelation. The Second Person of the

You Don't Have to Go It Alone

Trinity is called a True and Faithful Witness.

Writing to Jewish readers whose Scripture said, "In the mouth of two or three witnesses shall every word be established," in certain instances Matthew reports the healing of two, whereas other Gospels mention only one: two demons (Matthew 8:28; see Mark 5:2; Luke 8:27); and two blind men on two occasions (Matthew 9:27; 20:30; see Mark 10:46; Luke 18:35). When a person makes a motion in a business session, the person who seconds or "twos" it, strengthens the hand of the first person. In fact, each strengthens the other.

Ever notice how often the Lord used people two by two? Comments John Broadus in *Commentary on Matthew*, about Jesus' sending of the Twelve by twos, "This arrangement may possibly have been suggested by the fact that there were among the Twelve two or three pairs of brothers, but it had also some important advantages, both as regards the apostles themselves and as to their work. The two served as company for each other, preventing the loneliness which the Apostle Paul took so many pains to avoid on his journeys. They could also relieve each other in preaching which, in the open air and to the crowds gathered by their miracles, would be laborious, as our Lord Himself found it. And then the testimony of the two witnesses concerning the teachings and miracles of the Great Prophet who was coming after them would be more impressive among the people than that of one alone."[2]

When the Seventy were commissioned, again it was by twos (Luke 10:1). Jesus dispatched two disciples to get the colt for His Jerusalem entry (Mark 11:1,2), and two (perhaps the same duet) to make arrangements for the Passover in the upper room (Mark 14:13).

The Lord's servants worked often in pairs. To find out

14

if Jesus were the Messiah, John the Baptist sent two of his disciples (Matthew 11:2). The body of Jesus was buried by two Sanhedrinists, Joseph and Nicodemus, an act which would require the reinforcing encouragement of each other (John 19:38-42). Two disciples traveled the Emmaus road together (Luke 24:13-27). Going together to the temple to pray, Peter and John shared in the healing of a man lame from birth (Acts 3:1-8). When Dorcas died, the believers at Lydda sent two of their number to Joppa to ask Peter to come (Acts 9:38). Cornelius sent two of his household servants, along with a devout soldier, to urge Peter to come and preach to the centurion's household at Caesarea (Acts 10:7,8). The first missionaries commissioned by a church (Antioch) comprised a two-man team, Barnabas and Paul (Saul, Acts 13:2,3). When they parted ways because of strong contention, they formed two twosomes: Barnabas and Mark, and Paul and Silas (Acts 15:39,40). It was the latter two who were arrested together, beaten together and who sang praises together in the Philippian jail (Acts 15:19-25).

As Richard Wilbur so eloquently states in the poem, "Opposites":

> What is the opposite of two?
> A lonely me, a lonely you.[3]

The fellowship enjoyed by two may be enhanced by the addition of others. Three or more is not a crowd. The Master had an inner three, Peter, James, and John, whom He had close to Him on certain occasions, such as at the raising of Jairus' daughter (Luke 8:41,51); at the Transfiguration (Mark 9:2); and in Gethsemane (Mark 14:32,33). Apparently this number was augmented by

15

You Don't Have to Go It Alone

Andrew at times (Mark 13:3). And of course our Lord's basic group numbered twelve.

The partnership of Paul and Silas expanded into a team including at one time or other such men as Timothy, Luke, Tychicus, Epaphroditus, Demas, and Aristarchus (Acts 18:5; Ephesians 6:21; Philippians 2:25; Philemon 24). Though evangelistic leaders of the past century have been known in pairs—Moody and Sankey, Torrey and Alexander, Sunday and Rodeheaver, Graham and Barrows—each of these pairs gathered a larger team about them in their work.

A small group of six to twelve people meeting together informally in homes provides an ideal structure for effective fellowship. Lacking church buildings during the first two centuries, the saints probably met mostly in private homes. Today, large sanctuaries permit meetings of the entire membership of a church. Christian growth and renewal would seem to require the instruction and inspiration that come from both the corporate services and the small groups.

Howard A. Snyder in *The Problem of Wine Skins* says, "In fact, the use of the small groups of one kind or another seems to be a common element in all significant movements of the Holy Spirit throughout church history. Early Pietism was nurtured by the *collegio pietatis,* or house meetings for prayer, Bible study and discussion. The small group was a basic aspect of the Wesleyan Revival in England, with the proliferation of John Wesley's 'class meetings.' Small groups undergirded the Holiness Revival that swept America in the late 1800s and led, in part, to the modern Pentecostal movement. More significantly, the road to the Reformation was paved by small-group Bible studies. If nothing more, these facts surely suggest that small groups are conducive to a reviving ministry."[4]

May not the small groups find sanction in the words of Jesus? "Where two or three are gathered together in my name, there am I in the midst of them" (Matthew 18:20).

It's true, in some experiences we must go it alone. But lonely events can be made more bearable by the nearness and warmth of another. Gethsemane with its agonies would have been more bearable for Christ had the disciples watched and prayed instead of falling asleep. Jesus had chosen the disciples "that they should be with him," not only for casual curriculum but for compassionate company (Mark 3:14).

BELIEVERS BENEFIT EACH OTHER

When believers are seen blended together in the unity of Christ, not isolated by perforations of one kind or another, what a benefit to each other! The eye has need of the ear, as does the hand of the feet. Paul says, ". . . the members should have the same care one for another" (I Corinthians 12:25). A lady who moved from a distance said to her new pastor, "I would like to come under the watchcare of the church." The welcoming covenant of one church read, "We promise to watch over you with Christian fidelity and tenderness, ever treating you in love as members of the body of Christ."

Sometimes we emphasize our relationship to God to the neglect of our responsibilities to fellow believers. When the vertical relationship dominates our horizontal relationships we may forget our place as members of the body of Christ. The New Testament is full of reminders of our duties to one another. Here is a fairly exhaustive list in the order in which they appear:

17

You Don't Have to Go It Alone

—Have peace one with another (Mark 9:50).

—Love one another (John 13:34; 15:12,17; Romans 13:8; I Thessalonians 3:12; 4:9; I Peter 1:22; I John 3:11,23; 4:7; II John 5).

—In honor prefer one another (Romans 12:10).

—Be of the same mind one toward another (Romans 12:16).

—Judge not one another (Matthew 7:1; Romans 14:4).

—Edify one another (Romans 14:19).

—Receive one another (Romans 15:7).

—Admonish one another (Romans 15:14; Colossians 3:16).

—Greet one another (Romans 16:16; I Corinthians 16:20; II Corinthians 13:12; I Peter 5:14).

—Wait for one another (in partaking of the Lord's Supper) (I Corinthians 11:33).

—Care one for another (I Corinthians 12:25).

—Serve one another (Galatians 5:13).

—Do not consume, bite or devour one another (Galatians 5:15).

—Do not envy one another nor provoke to envy (Galatians 5:26).

—Bear one another's burdens (Galatians 6:2).

—Forbear one another (Ephesians 4:2; Colossians 3:13).

—Be kind one to another, tenderhearted (Ephesians 4:32).

—Forgive one another (Ephesians 4:32; Colossians 3:13).

—Submit to one another (Ephesians 5:21; I Peter 5:5).

—Lie not one to another (Colossians 3:9).

—Teach one another (Colossians 3:16).

—Exhort, comfort one another (same word in I Thessalonians 4:18; 5:11; Hebrews 3:13).

—Stir up one another to good works and love (Hebrews 10:24).

—Speak not evil one of another (James 4:11).

—Do not grumble against each other (James 5:9).

—Confess your faults one to another (James 5:16).

—Pray for one another (James 5:16).

—Practice hospitality to one another (I Peter 4:9).

—Minister (through gifts) one to another (I Peter 4:10).

Ever notice that the words for followers of Christ are so often in the plural? Saints, believers, disciples, brothers, Christians. An isolated Christian is a contradiction of terms.

Yet so many believers *feel* isolated. A Christian Distress Clinic in Toronto, Canada, which was started in 1974 primarily for evangelical believers who found it difficult to approach their pastors with their serious personal problems, reported over 6,000 telephone calls in the first two years of operation. Because many Christians are unable to relate easily to others, they found it helpful to be able to talk to another Christian on an anonymous, confidential basis without worrying whether the person on the other end of the line would accept him as a person.

The pastoral overseeing of the church does not belong exclusively to the shepherd of the flock. Each of us is his brother's keeper, and in a sense, an under-shepherd responsible to minister to others.

A young mother, an invalid, was lying on her bed when her nine-year-old daughter walked in. Seeing her mother reclining, she unfolded the blanket at the foot of the bed and gently tucked it around her mother.

"You know," her mother said, "it wasn't too long ago that I was tucking you in. And now here you are covering me up!"

19

You Don't Have to Go It Alone

The little girl bent over her mother and whispered, "We take turns," then slipped quietly out of the room.

The doctrine of the priesthood of believers requires us to serve each other. We are to be a brother to another, each for the other.

2
Bearing One Another's Burdens

When a workman's arm was struck by falling debris, his other arm automatically but tenderly seized the injured arm. His voice began to utter soothing words to the hurting member. His feet started shuffling around, and his back bent to a crouched posture. Instant reaction of other members of the body came to the rescue of the paining part.

This is how it should be in the body of Christ. The Apostle Paul wrote, "And whether one member suffer, all the members suffer with it" (I Corinthians 12:26). Along the same line he also commanded, "Bear ye one another's burdens" (Galatians 6:2).

In the original the order reads, "One another's burdens bear." The first, emphatic word is *one another's,* discouraging the self-centeredness of a father who prayed:

You Don't Have to Go It Alone

> "Lord, bless me and my wife,
> My son John and his wife,
> Us four and no more."

Or of a childless couple who prayed:

> "Lord, bless us two,
> And that will do."

Or of the bachelor:

> "Lord, bless only me,
> That's as far as I can see."

The second word is *burdens,* literally a weight, a wearisome toil to carry. Primary reference, according to context, is moral failure in which a believer has been overtaken (verse 1). But Paul probably meant the concept to include sickness, setbacks, and sorrows of all kinds, hard and heavy to be borne.

The final word in the text is *bear.* Christian love should help relieve a fellow believer when overtaxed by a crushing weight. A load is lighter when supported by two sets of shoulders. To be a people helper one must:

> be *there,*
> let another *share,*
> show *care,*
> offer *prayer,*
> then, in some appropriate way,
> his burden *bear.*

BE THERE

To whom do people go with a broken heart? Usually to a relative, associate, or close friend. Sometimes to a professional counselor or pastor. Hairdressers and barbers know what it is to have their shoulders cried on. A barber shop in a large city has two sections: one for those who wish to talk, and one for those who don't. The "talk" compartment has four partitions marked stock market, sports, general topics and family troubles.

A few years ago psychologist R. R. Carkhuff, while researching the effectiveness of lay-counselors, concluded that the patients of untrained people helpers did as well as or better than the patients of professionals.

The success of lay-counseling may be attributed to at least two factors: (1) The helper is closer to the person, thus better able to understand his problem and to work with him in its solution; (2) he is more accessible than the professional who requires one to come to his place at his time. The informality of the lay situation fosters easier communication and reduces tension.

This finding should not discourage the use of professionally trained counselors, but should encourage the exercise of helpful support by all believers. Probably more believers than realize it possess the gift of counseling, encouragement, showing mercy, burden-bearing. Who has better opportunity to help another than a fellow Christian? But he must be geographically near, accessible—even at unearthly hours. The potential burden-bearer must "be there."

LET ANOTHER SHARE

Though all have troubles, not everyone is willing to share his plight. When a young man lost his job, his wife noticed how people in the church acted embarrassed, smiled weakly, or avoided her in the hallway. Serving in the nursery one Sunday, she was asked by the other volunteer how things were going. At first replying with the usual amenities, she added that her husband was job hunting.

The volunteer responded with a slow, sad smile. "I know exactly what you're going through. We were in our ninth and final month of unemployment checks when my husband finally landed a job. We didn't know what we were going to do next." The young wife was not only surprised by the answer, but by the fact that "none of us in the church had known of their burden."

Many have been conditioned to keep their feelings within. Others are introverts by nature. Some don't wish to inflict additional burdens on others who already have plenty of their own. Still others feel their problems may become a topic of gossip. Pride may restrain a person from revealing a particular trial about his health, family or economic situation. For these and other reasons people make "unspoken" requests.

Though some matters are so private and personal or so potentially injurious to others that they should not be mentioned openly, far more sharing of adversity could be done than is practiced in many churches today. When members of the local family of God fail to help each other, those heavy with trouble will seek support elsewhere. Paul didn't hesitate to unveil his distresses, like his thorn in the flesh, and his being "an ambassador in bonds." No one can *bear* our pain unless we first *bare* that pain.

Though some dilemmas of others are evident to those who are alert and sensitive, other adversities will never be known unless the sufferer confides his desperation. When people asked a lady who had lost her husband in death how things were going, she said it took a lot of courage to tell the truth, "Things are *not* good. I'm very lonely. I need your love and friendship. Please come to the house for supper, or invite me to your home."

She asserted, "My friends helped me through some terrible times, but I had to stifle my pride, let them know I needed their help, and reach out for their strength."

Without sharing, there'll be no caring or bearing.

SHOW CARE

A bumper sticker bore the sign, "America's Greatest Problem is Apathy—But Who Cares?"

A mental hospital patient wrote,

> I am, yet what I am
> Who cares, or knows.
> My friends forsake me
> Like a memory lost.

An old sailor once gave this advice: "Don't tell your troubles to others. Most of them don't care a hang, and the rest are mighty glad of it." A proverb reads, "No man dies of another's wound." But Christians have been called to tend each other's wounds. This requires caring, and caring is displayed in many ways.

One way to show caring is listening. Listening to the troubled one unburden himself is preliminary to any burden-bearing. Non-listening betrays indifference, but hearing shows caring.

Listening takes concentration. Most people listen only part of the time with little interest. How easy it is for our eyes to stray or our mind to wander while thinking of our next interjection at the first sign of pause in the conversation.

The patient listener must give undivided attention, conveyed through eye contact, relaxed attitude, and remarks that show close interest such as, "I understand," or "Go on." Encouraged to converse about his problem in an atmosphere of quiet acceptance, friendly understanding, and empathic hearing, the troubled person often gains new perspective on his situation. At times he can free himself, get it off his chest completely and will exclaim in relief, "I feel better. My burden's not there now!" All because of a listening, caring person.

A missionary on deputation received word that her father had just passed away, whereupon her well-meaning pastor proceeded to give her a lecture on Christ's victory over death, complete with precise quotations of well-known verses. She later commented to others that her need at that moment was the solace of silence, not the semblance of a sermon.

Listening is a very important tool in the burden-bearer's kit.

Another way of showing caring is having compassion. When hearing of another's plight, our hearts should be moved with pity. Peter wrote, " . . . Be ye all of one mind, having compassion one of another, love as brethren, be pitiful, be courteous" (I Peter 3:8). Over and over again, the Lord Jesus was moved with compassion toward burdened folk.

In the Good Samaritan parable the robbers were not the only wicked ones; the real villains were the respected religious leaders who passed by without concern. Blind Helen Keller said, "The greatest pity is to see and not have vision." Too many have the gold-rush syndrome, the philosophy that one's mad dash to find wealth must keep him from stopping to help another in trouble lest that lost time cause another to beat him out in staking the best claim.

A pastor tells of an incident when he was a student for the ministry and was paid to help in the rehabilitation of an alcoholic, who when sober was worth thousands of dollars a year in his sales job. Young and full of energy, the ministerial student attended the man, but he didn't have enough influence to make him change. Years later the student, then a full-fledged pastor, returned to the old location to preach.

The former alcoholic, now an usher, took up the collection. In fact, he was a deacon also. Concluded the minister, "I had done no good because I was a hired hand. But his employer had learned to care for him, lived with him, and led him to Christ. He did what I didn't—got under him and helped bear his burden through compassion."

Sympathy has been defined as "feeling for another," "feeling from inside another's skin," and "two hearts tugging at one load." Everybody needs somebody he can weep with.

Seven-year-old Tom had to have his left arm amputated. When he returned to school his teacher gave the class an unusual assignment. She asked each child to tie his left arm behind his back. All morning the boys and girls were aware of the problems faced by Tom. Keeping paper from slipping while writing, turning the page of a book, putting on one's jacket, turning on a faucet and holding a glass at the same time were all awkward. The teacher taught the pupils empathy for Tom.

OFFER PRAYER

Believers sometimes make prayer covenants with

27

You Don't Have to Go It Alone

other believers to pray for each other daily. Burdens and answers to prayer can be shared by phone or over a cup of coffee. Many churches have a prayer chain which springs into operation immediately when an emergency arises. What a relief to the troubled person to know that hundreds are bearing him up before the throne of grace!

One church divided its membership into small groups for mutual prayer support. When a man died suddenly one midnight, the first people there were from the wife's prayer group. Even before calling her minister, the wife had turned to her prayer partners.

In another family, though the husband was a high-salaried executive, the marriage was coming unglued, the teenage son was on drugs, and the daughter was rebellious. A business move brought the family in contact with a church that grouped families two-by-two for prayer. Their assigned family radiated love between husband and wife, and between parents and children. The first family testified that it was the prayer of their new friends for and with them that brought their marriage back under the lordship of Christ.

John Wesley commented that through small group participation his followers began to bear each other's burdens and to naturally care more for each other, resulting in the experience of real Christian fellowship.

The Sunday night before Charles Colson pleaded guilty to the felony of obstructing justice, three other men joined him in his suburban home until well after midnight. Present in his den the night preceding his dramatic court appearance were his spiritual mentor ex-Senator Harold Hughes, former Texas Congressman Graham Purcell, and lay worker Douglas Coe. The purpose of the meeting was not to discuss whether Colson should plead guilty, for that he had already decided. The three gathered around Colson to give him moral and prayer support for his upcoming court ordeal.

BEAR THE BURDEN IN SOME
APPROPRIATE WAY

Often, tangible help is needed in order to actually bear another's burden. For example, James warned, "If a brother or sister be naked, and destitute of daily food, and one of you say unto them, Depart in peace, be ye warmed and filled; notwithstanding ye give them not those things which are needful to the body; what doth it profit?" (James 2:15,16). Genuine burden-bearing requires physical expression at times, in the giving of food or money, baby-sitting, housework, flat tire fixing, grocery shopping, chauffeuring, or some other down-to-earth assistance.

Francis Schaeffer said, "Most New Testament giving was to care for the material needs of other Christians." The early church shared so that no one had need (Acts 2:44,45; 4:34,35). Dorcas used her consecrated needle to sew garments for poor widows (Acts 9:39). Offerings were sent for the relief of starving brethren in Jerusalem by Gentiles in Antioch and in Europe (Acts 11:27-30; II Corinthians 11:8,9). James, Peter and John, in giving the right hand of fellowship to Paul and Barnabas for their ministry to the Gentiles, asked them to remember the poor (Galatians 2:9,10). The New Testament strongly urges giving "to the necessity of saints," and providing for "the fatherless and widows in their affliction" (Romans 12:13; James 1:27).

When rising unemployment caused increasingly more people to default on loans, a midwestern bank did not take a hard-nosed approach. Instead, the bank's executives attempted to get job-hunters together with employers who had jobs to fill.

Commenting on this incident, *Christianity Today* urged Christians in executive positions to do the same by setting up job clearinghouses. "Most of us know people who are unemployed: have we shown a desire to help them? Suggestions for job-hunting, a loan or gift of money if it's needed, a diverting evening for a couple who are experiencing hard times—these are some ways to say 'I care.' Many Christians seldom move beyond sympathy in bearing one another's burdens. How opportunities abound for acting upon the love God gives us."[5]

Perhaps the burden of prison needs to be relieved for some. Thinking of his own people who had been persecuted for their faith and in the process lost possessions and liberty, the writer of Hebrews wrote, "Remember them that are in bonds, as bound with them; and them which suffer adversity, as being yourselves also in the body" (Hebrews 13:3).

When Paul was incarcerated in the dreaded Mammertine prison in Rome, Onesiphorus often sought him out and refreshed the apostle, unashamed of his chains (II Timothy 1:16-18).

Bruce J. Lieske's article, "We Can Help Russian Believers," which appeared in *Missions Quarterly* (January, 1975), outlines the history of harassment of Russian believers, affirming that most Christians do not realize that the church has probably been persecuted more in the last fifty years behind the Iron, Bamboo and Sugar Cane Curtains than it ever was under the ancient Roman emperors. The article challenges Christians of the free world to help heal the wounds of a bleeding, martyred church by mourning for those who suffer, praying for them and sending financial help and Bibles.

Christian love should reach out to prisoners of all kinds, as the ministries of Chaplain Ray and Charles Colson do, for example. Who has not been thrilled with the story of *The Hiding Place* which tells how Corrie ten Boom saved the lives of numerous Jews from the Gestapo? Later, as an inmate of a concentration camp, she was able to share vitamins and medicine with weak and sickly prisoners.

Those who have lost a loved one, while deriving some comfort from a reminder of the glories of heaven now enjoyed by their departed loved ones, also need to unburden their grief-stricken hearts. Friends can listen to the outpouring of emotion, be sensitive to the bereaved's feelings, relate ways in which the departed has meant something to them, and pray with them. Says the Bible, "Rejoice with them that do rejoice, and weep with them that weep" (Romans 12:15).

Burden-bearing takes many forms. Neighbors stood around talking one evening. Conversation turned toward a new family in the development. An outspoken neighbor sounded off, "Well, what else can you expect when foreigners move in? Look, he's painted his front door red," whereupon one of the group walked to his garage and in a few minutes had painted his own front door bright red, also.

Though the Bible tells us to cast our cares on the Lord, God in heaven may seem remote to distraught humans. So the Lord has chosen to sustain us, often, through the kindness of other human beings, our fellow Christians.

Bearing others' burdens in no way implies ever-supporting psychological cripples, so that they never learn to handle their problems alone. Love may at times lead us to encourage burden-bearers to persevere through the resources of the indwelling Holy Spirit, thus contributing to their spiritual growth. Though love usually leads us to relieve a person of his problem, sometimes love can show him how to live with it.

Burdened people are all about us, many near the breaking point. A long illness has sapped someone's strength. A lengthy confinement has depleted the spirit of the niece taking care of her. A rebellious child has broken the heart of a parent. How sad when God's children fail to bear the weight of others' cares.

Helen Steiner Rice expresses this thought in her poem, "The World Would Be A Nicer Place If We Traveled At A Slower Pace":

> So what does it matter
>   if a man reaches his goal
> And gains the whole world
>   but loses his soul
> For what have we won
>   if in gaining this end
> We've been much too busy
>   to be *kind to a friend,*
> And what is there left
>   to make the heart sing
> When life is a *cold*
>   *and mechanical thing*
> And we are but puppets
>   of a controlled automation
> Instead of "joint heirs"
>   to *God's gift of creation.*[6]

Years ago the Salvation Army was holding an international convention which their founder, General William Booth, was too weak to attend. But he cabled his convention message to them. It was but one word—OTHERS.

3
Confessing One
to Another

Protestants have traditionally shied away from anything that resembles the confessional, mainly because the Bible emphasizes confessing our transgressions to God. However, the Bible also tells us, "Confess your faults [sins] one to another" (James 5:16).

Karl Menninger in his book, *Whatever Became of Sin?*, says that the early Christian church cells were comprised of small groups who met regularly, sometimes secretly, with an order of service which included self-disclosure and confession of sin. Confession was followed by an announcement of repentance and plans for restitution.

This practice continued until the time of Emperor Constantine who made Christianity the official state religion and instituted private confession to a priest, later depersonalized by the use of a confessional box.

The Reformation eliminated the confessional for its

You Don't Have to Go It Alone

followers, emphasizing direct confession to God. However, Moravian societies used to meet two or three times a week to confess their faults and pray for each other. Influenced by the Moravians, John Wesley instituted confession of sin in the early Methodist cells. In America, recent emphasis on small groups has enabled believers to revive the practice in an atmosphere of mutual honesty and trust.

WHAT IS CONFESSING?

The word *confess* (James 5:16) is made up of three parts which mean, in this order: out, the same, say. When the Lord convicts us that some course of action is wrong, we say the same in our heart (agree), then speak out our agreement for another to hear. Confession is agreeing with God's assessment in our inner soul, then speaking out openly about it to another or others. It is to say outwardly the same as God says inwardly.

Too often believers gloss over, instead of speaking out. We play a role, faking it when not making it, hiding from others, wearing a self-righteous mask to cover up inner spiritual warfare. One morning without notice, a lady called on her neighbor who exclaimed in bewilderment, "I'm so sorry you caught me looking my real self!" Instead of pretending all is well in our Christian lives, we often need to expose our true self and seek the healing that comes from the warmth and strength of real fellowship.

Corrie ten Boom in *Tramp for the Lord* tells how she and her traveling companion of many years learned to be honest with each other. It began with Conny, the companion, confiding in an older African Christian, "Tante Corrie is so much more mature than I. She has suffered much for Jesus, so when I see things in her life that are not right, I hesitate to speak them out to her."

The African believer answered, "That's not right. God has put you two together to help shed light on each other's path. She needs you and you need her."

That night with difficulty, Conny told Corrie some things in Corrie's life which Conny thought didn't glorify God. Corrie later admitted that it wasn't easy to hear the things she had done wrong but thought how wonderful it was that Conny had been honest.

Though Corrie apologized, it was still difficult for Conny to correct Corrie until one day the breakthrough came. In Argentina, about to leave Rio de Janeiro to fly to Buenos Aires, they discovered their suitcases overweight because of many presents. Corrie unpacked her luggage making three piles, one to send to Holland by sea, one to give to the poor in Rio, and the smallest to pack in her suitcase for the trip to Buenos Aires. Then Corrie hurried into Conny's room and began separating Conny's luggage into the same three piles, too busy to notice that Conny sat there quite silent.

A week later, walking together along a beautiful beach in Buenos Aires, Conny, in a strained voice, told Corrie, "I promised to be honest with you. I must get something settled. When you repacked my suitcase and decided which of my things to send to Holland, what to give to the poor, and what to leave for me, I was unhappy about it."

Corrie immediately apologized, "How stupid and tactless of me to rush in and interfere like that. Forgive me, please."

When silence followed for some time, Conny asked, "Are you unhappy, Corrie? You're so quiet." It was Corrie's turn to be honest.

You Don't Have to Go It Alone

"Yes, there's something bothering me. Why did you not tell me immediately that you were disturbed? Then it would have been settled on the spot and you wouldn't have had to carry this heavy burden all these days. From now on let's both speak the truth in love, and not let the sun go down on our misunderstandings."

Corrie ten Boom calls the above practice *walking in the light,* based on the verse, "But if we walk in the light, as he is in the light, we have fellowship one with another, and the blood of Jesus Christ his Son cleanseth us from all sin" (I John 1:7).

Paul often opened up his inner heart to reveal his struggles. He told of the conflict of his two natures, doing what he didn't want to do and failing to do what he wished to do. He also told both the Corinthians and the Thessalonians of his unrest of spirit when uncertain of their spiritual status, until a good report finally reached him (II Corinthians 2:13; I Thessalonians 3:5).

WHY CONFESS OUR SINS ONE TO ANOTHER?

Spiritual health requires that wrongdoing not be *suppressed,* but *expressed* to God, and if necessary, to man. However, not all confession of wrong to fellowman is healthy; exceptions will be given later in this chapter.

Confession helps to get the problem out of our system. If we keep our blunders within us, they fester, grow, and can cause psychosomatic illness. Others will ask, "What's eating you?" Repressed guilt does not die, but crops up indirectly through irritating cough, tight throat, indigestion, or headache. Swiss counselor Paul Tournier writes that people who come to him with physical complications are often suffering guilt of unconfessed wrongdoings which drain body resistance, thus increasing susceptibility

36

to various kinds of disease.

Believing that the heart was the seat of thought and emotion, medieval scholars said that a person burdened with guilt had a stained breast. Confession which brought relief was called making a clean breast of things.

King David relates the ill effects of failure to confess his sin. "When I kept silence (by not confessing), my bones wasted away." But when David made a clean breast of it to God, Nathan, and others, his pent-up burden was lifted. His relief is expressed in Psalms 32 and 51. Not without reason does James link confession and healing. "Confess your faults one to another, and pray one for another, that ye may be healed" (James 5:16). Confession is good for the soul—and the body.

Confession to a human being provides human affirmation of our forgiveness. Sometimes a person who confesses a sin to the Lord has difficulty believing he actually has been forgiven. But if he confides in a close Christian friend, an understanding person may help to reinforce the reality of God's forgiveness with a simple, reassuring word.

Of course, only God can forgive. The apostles never forgave sins, although when a person confessed his wrongdoing to the Lord, the apostles affirmed to him, on the basis of God's promise through the redemptive work of Christ, that his sins had been remitted (John 20:23). Though no human can forgive sin, a person can declare to a penitent the assurance of divine forgiveness.

It's true, "What a Friend We Have in Jesus," but it's also true that we need human friends at times. A visible friend can reinforce the fact of forgiveness given by the Invisible Friend.

A student for the ministry began to doubt his salvation because of a previous period of backsliding. He wrote a

You Don't Have to Go It Alone

Christian leader, admitting his wrongdoing, but also expressing fear as to whether God had remitted his sin. A return letter from the Christian leader containing the simple statement, "I believe with all my heart that God has put your sin behind His back," brought joy, confirmation of complete forgiveness, and a restoration of assurance of salvation which the student never lost thereafter.

Confession helps to make us humble. The three hardest words in the English language to say are, "I am sorry." To confess sin is a humiliating, searching, cleansing experience. Jim Vaus, criminal turned Christian youth worker, tells how right after his conversion, he tried to make restitution for every fraudulent deal he could remember. Each time he entered a place of business to admit a particular act of theft against that company and to offer repayment, Vaus experienced a sickening sensation in the pit of his stomach.

Though readily forgiven by most officials, the ordeal of exposing his wrongs tore at the vitals of his dignity. Especially difficult was confessing to the president of the Bible Institute of Los Angeles where he had once been a student that he had pilfered contributions from radio listeners while in charge of interoffice mail delivery.

A comedian who was a poor ice skater said that he seldom fell but had to do a lot of twisting, writhing and waving of hands to keep his balance. Perhaps in life it would be preferable not to look silly in our attempts to keep our feet on the ground, but to suffer a good fall and any resulting wounding of dignity. Admission of sin may hurt our pride but it provides an excellent opportunity for picking ourselves up and starting anew, which is more honest than giving the illusion of never falling.

Confession makes repetition of that wrongdoing more

38

difficult. Confession puts you "on the record" with those who hear your admission. The person who merely says within, "I'm not going to eat so much candy," may easily break the vow because no other human has heard it. But if that person goes on record, confessing gluttony in the matter of candy, it will be harder to eat candy in the open.

Confession encourages others to be honest. A new home Bible study group of neighborhood women dealt with the theme of patience. One of the finest Christian ladies blurted out that often she was impatient with her husband and children, even entertaining mean, hateful thoughts toward her family. Other women, unused to such openness, hid behind a pious front, suggesting they would pray for this impatient, unloving lady. On the surface this lady looked like a poor Christian, but her straightforwardness paid off later when others began to share some of their unkind thoughts and words, and to find support in the prayers of each for the other.

A man confided in a friend that he had been having a certain problem for years. The friend replied, "In all the years we've been pals I had the impression you never had any problems. So often I wanted to confide in you, but you seemed so cheerful around church that I thought you wouldn't understand me."

When Paul uncovered his inner conflicts, his vulnerability let his readers see the living Christ at work in his life, thus giving them courage in their struggles. Do not David's Psalms of defeat, despair and frustration buoy us up hundreds of years later as we enter into his experience of depression, then find relief?

WHEN NOT TO CONFESS TO ONE ANOTHER

Mark Twain reportedly said, "Everybody is a moon,

and has a dark side which he never shows to anybody." And it could be added, "which he should never show to anybody." Here are some cases where privacy should be maintained.

When confession would needlessly damage one's reputation it should not be confessed to another human. Mark Twain also called confession "good for the soul and bad for the reputation."

The late Dr. Donald Grey Barnhouse relates two cases of embezzlement which he treated differently. The first involved a man who was sent to prison for stealing several hundred dollars. On his release he confessed his sin in a public meeting of the church where he had been a member, also stating his determination to live a moral life with God's help. He took a job at menial work, laboring manfully until a much better position opened up.

The other man embezzled about the same amount, but before any detection occurred, in desperation he contacted Dr. Barnhouse who was able to work out a plan to rehabilitate the young man without any public disclosure. His manager quietly transferred him to a position where he would not handle money. In due time he repaid the loan which had enabled him to replace the amount he had stolen. Later he was promoted to a position of trust.

Dr. Barnhouse insisted that public confession would have been disastrous for him. Furthermore, he advised the young banker that no pressure from any spiritual leader should make him feel he should mention it publicly, for it was strictly a private matter. Of course, if years later he felt divulgence could bring spiritual help to someone, it would then be permissible to mention it.

Confession need not be any more public than the knowledge of the act. Reports of sin should not be circulated or published for the public's general consumption and discussion. Usually only those directly involved need be informed of a confession.

One should not confess to another person when it would harm another's reputation. How unwise to give unsympathetic people unnecessary fodder for gossip. Even in a circle of understanding, intimate friends, we should take care not to expose an innocent outside party without his permission.

Some years ago in a wave of public confession meetings held in fine hotels and on great estates, many from high society strata began baring their souls to each other. In many instances public confession did great harm to other people involved in the episodes, for sin is not a matter that always involves one person alone. Dirty linen, ours or others', should not be flaunted on the line for all to see.

It is not wise to confess to another person when confession becomes bragging. A Hollywood columnist, induced to attend a confession meeting, wrote with great irony that at last he had found the type of religion he could go for in a big way. For, he explained, the next best thing to committing a sin is in telling about it afterwards. He pointed out that a man could sin his way through manhood, then when he was old and worn out he could go to a confession meeting and live all his sinful moments over again in the telling, while wide-eyed little lads looked at him in wonder and admiration, as they would look at the champion of any sport.

Nor should confession be made when it would needlessly hurt the person confessed to, the confessee. At a college week of special services the evangelist exhorted students to confess to anyone if they had anything against that person. The Greek professor, a timid lady who graded hard, was deeply embarrassed when a line of near-

41

ly a dozen students formed in front of her to tell her how much they hated her. (Who knows how long the line would have been had there been a course in Hebrew!) The above confession amounted to insult.

It is a poor time to confess one's sin when such a confession would encourage or make light of sin. Dr. Robert K. Rudolph, Reformed Episcopal Seminary professor, wrote in *Christian Heritage:* "Confession of one's faults according to James 5:16 was cited by the Buchmanites as the Scripture's warrant for their practice. However, in the course of time, the confession of particular and spectacular sins of an immoral nature became such a cause of increasing immorality, that even secular colleges began to ban Buchmanites from their campuses. There are always many people around who find the discussion of immorality stimulating or amusing, and there is always among sinners a tendency to outdo one another in the telling of 'tall' tales. Actually, though such endeavors may be born of a basic desire to glorify the Lord, such a practice will soon be an enticement to the wicked enjoyment of pornographic vicarious experiences—not only written, but spoken."[7]

Confession of wrongdoing should be balanced by Paul's injunction, "For it is a shame even to speak of those things which are done of them in secret" (Ephesians 5:12). Often, ventilating our sinful deeds makes them seem less wicked. Also, when we are carelessly broadcasting data on our sinful exploits, we will not be thinking of things that are pure and lovely (Philippians 4:8), nor will we be helping our hearers to think on an elevated plane.

If relating a misdeed would give excuse or encouragement to another to follow suit, refrain. Confession can sow germs of suggestion and moral disease in the minds of others. Only when confession would help, not hinder, should such be shared.

No one has the right to demand another to unfold the secrets of his heart, except in the need for discipline. When evidence shows dishonesty, the individual must then be made to confess and restore any loss as far as possible.

HOW TO CONFESS

Spontaneously. Confession must not be perfunctory, expected every Friday or every time the small group meets. It should not be forced at a formal time and place but should be free, not out of habit but out of the heart.

Reciprocally. Confession is not a one-way street; rather, it is a mutual matter. Though some will confess at one time with others hearing, in time all will have confessed and all will have heard. Bishops, elders or deacons are not instructed to be the hearers of the members. Nor are officers told to confess only to officers. Christians are all on an equal footing, both as to susceptibility to and admission of sin. Confession may be made to one another without the distinction of rank.

Specifically. Too often we fail in true confession by making our confession too general. When we vaguely own up to our failures, we escape responsibility for any particular matter. We need to confess the exact area in which we failed; not, "Lord, forgive me for not witnessing more," but, "Lord, I had a golden opportunity to witness to my neighbor this morning when we both were hanging out our wash. Forgive me, and help me next time we are together by ourselves to give a faithful witness."

Penitently. Not only must we confess our sin; we must do it in the spirit of repentance—not like the fellow who

43

confessed to his minister that he had stolen a bale of straw the night before, then added, "No, make it two bales, for I intend to steal another one tonight." We must not only make affirmation of our wrong, but we must show the spirit of determination to change and follow the right way of life. The old way must be discarded and a new way followed.

Trustfully. Preferably, confessions should be made in a circle of friends clothed by a maximum of trust. We need sympathetic listeners who will keep our confidence, who will cover up our confessed faults, not think less of us for whatever deed we confess. Such kindness is found mainly where people have a close, brotherly relationship. Where trust is lacking, revelation of wrong may elicit criticism.

Confession by a fellow saint should lead the hearer to pray for him. "Confess your faults one to another, and pray one for another" (James 5:16). Since no Christian is infallible, every believer needs the support of fellow believers. Not criticism, scolding or brutal frankness, but loving, tender care and prayer.

At a college conference at Forest Home Christian Conference Grounds in California some years ago, 600 students gathered in outdoor Victory Circle for prayer and testimony. Director Dr. Henrietta Mears impressed the students with the need for honesty with God and submission to His will. One young man, a six-foot, husky football player, began to weep uncontrollably. He confessed to living a lie since his return from World War II. He claimed to be a hero who had shot down several enemy planes, when in reality he now admitted he had been washed out in flight school, spending the war years on the ground repairing damaged planes. His large frame shook. He slumped to the ground, face in the dust, sobbing and asking the Lord to forgive him.

Two nights later he dedicated his life to the ministry. Some years later many of the same friends who had heard his confession of duplicity saw his dedication come to fruition in his ordination to the ministry.

What we have to confess may not be as major as this case. Nor should we confess imaginary sin, the product of an overly sensitive conscience. But when properly handled, confession will be good for the soul—ours and others'!

4
Receiving One Another

An unusual prayer meeting was held awhile ago in Washington, D. C. by four men with drastically different backgrounds: ex-"hatchet" lawyer, Republican Charles Colson; former alcoholic, Democrat ex-Senator Harold Hughes; former Black Panther Minister of Information, Eldridge Cleaver; and a Ku Klux Klanner serving time for violence against blacks, now involved in Colson's Prison Fellowship ministry.

Despite racial, political, and social dissimilarities, these four found fellowship through a common forgiveness. Their acceptance of each other obeyed Paul's command to first-century believers of varying viewpoints: "Wherefore receive ye one another" (Romans 15:7). Because they have been united in Christ's body, Christians of all people should extend a warm welcome to one another.

SOME DIFFERENCES LOVE SHOULD
TRANSCEND

Love should transcend the differences of cultural practices or lifestyles. Due to widespread idolatry, most meat sold in Rome's marketplace had been first offered to idols in temples. Trained to loathe idols, believing Jews insisted that Gentile Christians refrain from such meat. But most Gentile believers, while rejecting idol worship, correctly discerned nothing immoral with eating meat offered to idols. How could the offering of meat before a piece of carved wood or stone affect the meat? they questioned. So they ate meat whenever they wished. The situation was potentially explosive. The abstainers (called the weak), and the eaters (termed the strong), were already engaged in mutual censure and unkind judgment.

Paul advised, "Him that is weak in the faith receive ye, but not to doubtful disputations. For one believeth that he may eat all things: another, who is weak, eateth herbs. Let not him that eateth despise him that eateth not . . ." (Romans 14:1-3).

We are to welcome any brother to the faith who wants to join us, if his faith is genuine, and we are not to disparage his viewpoints on minor matters when they do not agree with ours.

Disagreement prevails today in evangelical circles over various practices. For instance, some Christians from the South may frown on mixed swimming, while others may think nothing of lighting up a cigarette. In some areas, wearing a wedding ring is considered worldly, whereas people in other localities think failure to wear a ring invites illicit flirtation. Some groups forbid lipstick but permit the use of powder. One lady told a women's missionary society that it was wrong to wear earrings, but as she spoke three strands of pearls encircled her neck.

Evangelical Christians readily reject the lifestyles clearly forbidden in the Bible, such as premarital sex and

47

homosexuality. In the area of questionable practices William Barclay writes in his *Letters to Romans* that many a congregation has been "torn in two because those who hold broader and more liberal views are angrily contemptuous of those whom they regard as stick-in-the-mud, die-hard conservatives and puritans; and because those who are stricter in their outlook are critical, censorious, and condemning of those who wish the right to do things which they think are wrong."[8]

The situation at the church in Rome had advanced to the point where some members wanted to bar membership to those who held differing views. Paul had some advice in this chapter, Romans 14, for both the strong and the weak.

To the strong: "Do not despise the weak." Weak believers should be welcomed into membership. The church is not a place for perfect people but a school for the spiritually illiterate to learn, and a hospital for the spiritually ill to be made whole. The weak should be received without engaging them in "doubtful disputations" (verse 1), disputing over opinions.

To the weak: "Do not judge the strong." Though the tendency of the strong is to scorn the weak, the temptation of the abstainer is to judge the "eater." Too often the weak wish to make others conform to their standards. This playing God opens one up to glaring inconsistency.

A lady spent ten minutes telling a friend she shouldn't wear makeup, wedding rings or lipstick, then when she was about to leave added, "By the way, I see your hair is getting gray on the side. Why don't you touch it up with some dye? I'll tell you the brand I use."

Under the lordship of Christ, each person must decide for himself. Since situations vary, conclusions may differ on debatable items. Conviction of the heart, not convention of the crowd, should dictate one's behavior. "Let every man be fully persuaded in his own mind"(verse 5).

Again to the strong: "Respect the weak brother's conscience." Paul warns the strong against flaunting his liberty, for it may encourage a weak brother to violate his conscience, a snare in the path of spiritual progress. Paul commands that "no man put a stumblingblock or an occasion to fall in his brother's way." He also states, "It is good neither to eat flesh, nor to drink wine, nor any thing whereby thy brother stumbleth" (verses 13,21).

Again to the weak: "Grow up." Paul uses the term, "weaker brother," for the person who has scruples and demands that others live by them. (A scruple is an opinion without concrete Biblical support, like the judgment that men should wear white shirts to church.) Faith is feeble when it confuses lifestyle with Christian duty, or equates sports, fashions, or guitars with love, mercy and purity. Weaker brethren who get uptight over certain questionable practices should ask the Lord for grace to develop into healthy, robust believers.

A young woman confessed, "When I was first converted, I honestly thought all Christian girls should wear their dresses to their ankles, long hair down their backs, and always carry a Bible. I was even indignant when I saw Christians reading secular books. The Lord soon began to remind me that all Christendom wasn't required to live up to my pious standards! I had to surrender my self-righteous attitudes and realize that God was more concerned with a person's heart attitudes. Nothing is wrong with dresses down to the ankle or with carrying a Bible everywhere, but every Christian doesn't have to do it."

Love should transcend the differences of nationality. Difference in lifestyle in the early church was often accentuated by difference in race, for the abstainer from meat

You Don't Have to Go It Alone

was usually a Jew, while the eater was Gentile. A strong line of demarcation ran between Jew and Gentile all through the Roman Empire. Though their houses were next to each other, and though they mingled freely in the market, a Jew would not eat with a Gentile nor enter his house.

Peter, a Jew, said to Cornelius, a Gentile, "It is an unlawful thing for a man that is a Jew to keep company, or to come unto one of another nation . . ." (Acts 10:28). (Peter later relented this opinion, once God had shown him in a vision it was not His will for such a division to exist.) Strong animosity also existed between Jews and Samaritans.

How could these hostile barriers be overcome? On the cross Jesus died for Jew, Samaritan and Gentile. At Pentecost the Holy Spirit fused 3,000 Jewish believers into one body. Then the Holy Spirit reached out to the Samaritans, then Gentiles, placing them in the same body of Christ.

"Aliens from the commonwealth of Israel" were now made one with the Jew. Paul wrote, "For he is our peace, who hath made both one, and hath broken down the middle wall of partition between us; Having abolished in his flesh the enmity . . . And that he might reconcile both unto God in one body by the cross" (Ephesians 2:14-16).

Thereafter, differences were irrelevant, for in Christ we are neither Jew nor Gentile. Believers were to receive each other as brothers in the Lord and in the companionship of the cross.

Psychologist Gordon Allport in his book, *The Nature of Prejudice,* claims that no corner on earth is free from racial bias. He points out that at one time some West Indies nationals would hold their nose conspicuously when passing an American on the street. Germans called their eastern neighbors "Polish cattle," whereas the Poles retaliated with "Prussian swine." In South Africa, it was said that the English were against the Afrikaner, both were against the Jew, all three were opposed to the Indians, while all four conspired against the national black.

But among believers all racial differences should be overcome by the gospel which places all nations in the circle of divine love. On a body-strewn battlefield toward the end of World War I a wounded Frenchman gave a wounded German a drink of water out of the Frenchman's bottle. Both were Christians. After the German finished drinking, the Frenchman took his hand and was heard to say, "There shall be no more war over there." Moments later both collapsed in death.

Love should transcend the differences of political philosophy. The disciples espoused a wide range of political outlooks. Matthew had been a tax collector, a profession scorned as turncoat because they worked hand-in-hand with the despised Roman authorities, earning themselves classification with the scum of society—"publicans and sinners." On the opposite side of the political spectrum was Simon who belonged to the Zealots, a fanatic Jewish party whose aim was liberation from Roman oppression. How could such extremes, an accused pro-Romanist and an avowed anti-Romanist, coexist in the same little band? Yet, throughout the earthly ministry of Jesus, and after the resurrection, too, the apostles maintained cohesiveness. Jesus allowed maximum individuality by fusing strong personalities into harmony.

Today, believers of differing political ideologies such as Democrats and Republicans should be able to fellowship in the same church.

Love should transcend differences of financial or social status. A famous architect related a costly blunder. One

51

busy morning a stranger in a baggy suit and slouch hat was ushered into his office. He wanted the architect to design a new porch, as his old one was in bad shape.

"Poor old man, probably living in some hovel he wants repaired," thought the architect as he promptly forgot the request. Twice in the next month the old man showed up, and twice the architect put the matter out of his mind.

Then one day the most important architectural job of the decade was awarded to a rival architect. The president of the insurance company who had made the announcement was mentioned in the newspaper. Rummaging through his desk, the architect found the card of the poor old man who had wanted his porch fixed. The name on the card was the same as the president of the major insurance company.

The Bible forbids dealing with a person on the superficial basis of outward appearance. James draws a picture of a church service into which walks a well-to-do visitor, dressed in costly clothes and wearing a gold ring. Immediately an usher moves this distinguished visitor to a seat of honor. Moments later the door opens again, this time revealing a shabbily dressed man from the poor class. No usher moves in his direction, but finally someone points to an inconspicuous corner.

James forbids such face-receiving. We are to welcome one another without regard for financial or social status (James 2:1-4). Four college students on an assignment for a sociology class, dressed in sweaters, jeans and running shoes, visited several churches Sunday evenings. Half the churches refused them admission, while the other half let them in begrudgingly.

During the days of student rebellion in the '60s, a church in Berkeley, California, always ended its service with the same hymn. The assistant pastor, seeing hippie-dressed young people walking by the open door, often wondered if the young people didn't smile at the words of the song as it floated outdoors: "Just as I am."

Does the average church more easily welcome someone well-dressed, well-educated, and well-heeled? We are not to acquiesce to the important and slight the seemingly inconsequential.

Paul suggested to Philemon that he receive runaway slave Onesimus as he would welcome Paul (Philemon 12). What grace it would have taken for a first-century master to accept back a slave, especially one who had stolen from him.

A feature of early church life was the love feast, a complete meal eaten prior to the Lord's Supper each Sunday evening. The rich were expected to provide most of the food. Their sharing enabled the poor to enjoy at least one bountiful meal a week. However, at Corinth, what was meant to foster the spirit of brotherliness became corrupted through selfishness. Some rich ate all or most of what they brought, resulting in the poor going hungry or eating leftovers. One can almost see the wealthy sitting by themselves, feasting on an abundance of dainties, disregarding the poor who were forced to sit by themselves with their bowl of watery soup.

Paul's remedy was not to abolish the meal. His practical solution was to advise the Corinthians to "tarry one for another," thus eliminating hasty schismatic eating. Paul said it would be preferable to eat at home before coming, rather than devouring one's food like a famished animal. Eating selfishly was unworthy of Him who gave His body and shed His blood unselfishly (I Corinthians 11:20-22,33). "The rich and poor meet together: the Lord is the maker of them all" (Proverbs 22:2).

Every church has its share of misfits, mentally slow,

53

physically handicapped, socially unaware, and poor. Someone has suggested that the Lord puts a few in every congregation to provide opportunity for the more blessed to grow by accepting and loving the less fortunate.

Love should transcend differences in doctrinal non-essentials. One day Disciple John told Jesus that he had stopped a man casting out demons in Jesus' name because the man was not one of Jesus' followers (Mark 9:38-40). When Jesus answered, "Forbid him not," He was in effect saying, "Even though he is not one of our group like you, John, he is nevertheless occupied in the same cause. By casting out demons he is uplifting My name."

Jesus' comment, "For he that is not against us is on our part" (verse 40), warns against a spirit of exclusiveness which would restrict the use of our gifts and graces to our own private company, and would rule out those who don't believe or serve just as we do. Narrowness may seek the promotion of our own group rather than Christ's glory. Those we condemn may well be doing Christ's work, also.

On another occasion Jesus gave the maxim in reverse, "He that is not with me is against me" (Matthew 12:30). Together these apothegms teach the impossibility of neutrality towards Jesus Christ, for we are either for or against Him. Perhaps when judging ourselves, we can apply the tougher, "If I'm not with Him, I'm against Him." And when evaluating others, we can take the gentler, "If he's not against Christ, he's with Him."

A Christian should not speak of fellow believers as if they were detached from him. A "we" versus "they" attitude is as incongruous as one's hand regarding itself as independent of the heart that pumps blood to it. We should avoid divisive and derisive terminology in describing fellow believers.

Welcoming another, however, does not extend to those who deny vital, fundamental Christian truth. Paul did not hesitate to call "accursed" anyone who preached other than the gospel of grace (Galatians 1:8). Nor did John fail to warn against giving support to anyone propagating false teaching about Christ (II John 9,10). On the other hand, we should be cautious lest we classify as non-brothers in the Lord those who don't dot their "i's" and cross their "t's" exactly as we do on fine doctrinal points.

INCENTIVES FOR RECEIVING ONE ANOTHER

All believers have been made one in Christ. Christians have been baptized by the Spirit into one body, possess a common salvation, have escaped a common danger, and have found a common refuge, like the animals who found safety in Noah's ark.

Imagine the unfriendly remarks that could have been made by animals as they approached the ark. Those with stripes perhaps weren't keen on associating with those with spots. The speedy hare could have criticized the slow-moving turtle. Imagine that a dark-colored bird advocated black power, while a light-colored heron stood for white supremacy. But when the sky darkened, probably all quit arguing. When the rain began to fall, all the beasts, including wolf and lamb, scurried up the gangplank together. Likewise, Christianity makes possible fellowship between people who otherwise could not tolerate each other.

Areas of differences are not the basics in Christianity. Paul wrote that "the kingdom of God is not meat and drink" (Romans 14:17). He could have added, nor rings nor cosmetics, nor fashions, nor hairstyles, nor Gentile,

55

nor Jew, nor Democrat, nor Republican, nor wealth, nor intelligence.

One Sunday morning decades ago in Washington, D.C., Chief Justice Charles Evans Hughes walked to the front of a Baptist church to receive the right hand of fellowship, and found himself standing beside a washer-woman, a little boy, and an Oriental. Looking at the four new members, the pastor remarked to the congregation, "Before the cross the ground is level." What is basic, Paul added in Romans 14:17, is "righteousness, and peace, and joy in the Holy Ghost."

We should receive one another because of the transcendent glory of Christ. James warned that discrimination was the wrong way to display belief in the Lord Jesus Christ, for He is the Lord of glory (James 2:1). In the blazing brilliance of the Son of God all differences and degrees of rank fade into nothingness. Just as both bright and dim stars disappear before the rising sun, so human distinctions—millionaire and pauper, mentally gifted and mentally slow, black and white, king and com-moner—evaporate into nothingness before the dazzling splendor of the Son of Righteousness. In the light of Christ's glory, how can any believer be guilty of fawning-ly seeking the company of a fellow believer just because he is chairman of the board, or a celebrity, or a con-gressman, while at the same time snubbing those who hold lesser positions? Such bootlicking ruptures the law of love.

Though a vital church growth principle holds to the "homogeneous unit," namely that churches grow best where membership is composed of "our kind of people," shouldn't the New Testament ideal embrace all kinds in any local church, not just those of the same culture who feel comfortable when together?

We Christians should receive one another because of Jesus' example. Despite being born into a fiercely nationalistic empire chafing under the hated Roman oppressor, and despite rigid segregation from Samaritans, Jesus Christ displayed not the slightest trace of prejudice, intolerance, bigotry, or racism. He reached out to all groups, specifically sinners. So we are told to "receive ye one another, as Christ also received us" (Romans 15:7).

At a Christmas program a six-year-old handicapped boy was attempting his first recitation. As he walked across the platform with great struggle, an older boy called out a disparaging remark about the lad's handicap. Completely demoralized, the little boy just stood and sobbed. A man rose from his seat, walked to the platform, knelt beside the boy, and put his arm around him. Then he said to the audience, "It takes a very cruel person to say what was just said to this little boy. He is suffering from something not his fault in any way. This was his first time to venture out with his handicap to say something in public. He has been hurt deeply. But I want you to know that this little boy is mine. I love him just the way he is. He belongs to me and I am proud of him."

Then he led the lad off the platform. Since Christ welcomes us as we are, we should extend a similar welcome to all our brothers in Christ.

We should receive one another in spite of any differences because differences may complement each other. Full-time pastors need the help of part-time laymen. Career missionaries must recognize the place of short-termers. Bible teachers must appreciate the ministry of gospel musicians. Remember Paul's rhetorical questions: "If the whole body were an eye, where were the hearing? If the whole were hearing, where were the smelling?" (I Corinthians 12:17). Differences in the body of Christ

You Don't Have to Go It Alone

make it possible for the entire body to function smoothly.

In a Swiss town nestled at the foot of a mountain stands a monument with two figures. One is a famous personality, a cultured scientist and author of many books; the other, a poor Swiss peasant and humble Alpine guide. This monument shows the dependence of greatness upon mediocrity, for the scientist could never have scaled the mountain without the lowly guide. Fittingly, both figures are included in the monument. How often the differences in people's disciplines provide the know-how and strength to accomplish a task which could not have been achieved alone.

Acceptance brings warmth to the whole fellowship. In his book *Leadership,* Dr. Hudson Armerding, president of Wheaton College, relates an incident that occurred one morning when he was scheduled to speak in chapel. As Wheatonites gathered prior to the service to ask the Lord's blessing, a young man with a beard and long hair, a sash around his waist and sandals walked in.

Says Dr. Armerding, "As I looked at him, I was sorry he had come in. Worse yet, he sat down right beside me. When we went to prayer, I did not enter into the praying with a very good attitude.

"Then the young man began to pray, and his prayer went something like this: 'Dear Lord, you know how much I admire Dr. Armerding, how I appreciate his walk with you. I am so grateful for what a man of God he is, and how he loves you and loves your people. Lord, bless him today. Give him liberty in the Holy Spirit and make him a real blessing to all of us in the student body. Help us to have open hearts to hear what he has to say, and may we just do what you want us to do.'

"As I walked down the steps to go into the chapel, the Lord spoke to me about my attitude. After giving my message, I asked the young man to come to the platform. Later I learned that one of the students turned to another and remarked that I was probably about to dismiss the young man from school as an example to the rest of the students.

"Thus, everyone including the young man was surprised when I put my arms around him and embraced him as a brother in Christ. That broke up the chapel service. Students stood and applauded; they cried and embraced each other. The reaction was unprecedented, and under God seemed to change the mood on campus to one of greater love and acceptance of one another.'"

5
Forgiving One Another

Clara Barton, founder of the American Red Cross, was once reminded of an especially unkind act that had been done to her years before. But Miss Barton could not seem to recall it. When her friend asked, "Don't you remember it?" The reply came, "I distinctly remember forgetting that incident."

Too often people do not forget unkind deeds done to them. Rather, they retaliate. And so quarrels happen. When a spirit of rancor develops in our hearts, causing a leakage of divine power, anger, threats, malice and recrimination often follow.

But it shouldn't be that way. Paul wrote to the Ephesians, "Let all bitterness, and wrath, and anger, and clamour, and evil speaking, be put away from you, with all malice: And be ye kind one to another, tenderhearted, forgiving one another, even as God for Christ's sake hath forgiven you" (Ephesians 4:31,32).

60

To the Colossians Paul advised, "Forbearing one another, and forgiving one another, if any man have a quarrel against any: even as Christ forgave you, so also do ye" (Colossians 3:13). The word *quarrel,* occurring only here in the New Testament, means *occasion of complaint.*

Forgiveness requires certain qualities, not only at the point of its granting, but before and after.

IN THE PERIOD BEFORE FORGIVENESS

Harbor no bitterness. Sometimes tragedy makes people see the stupidity of holding resentment. When the San Francisco earthquake of 1906 caused buildings to reel for 45 seconds, a man ran out on Market Street, met, and shook hands with a man he had refused to speak to for ten years.

Besides being an indication of spiritual wrong, harboring grudges can have disastrous physical effects. A Christian lady who suffered severe headaches asked help from her doctor. Questioning revealed strong irritation against her non-believing husband for bringing trashy magazines into the living room to deliberately annoy her. Her doctor advised her to follow the example of Christ who prayed for His tormentors. Through the help of the indwelling Holy Spirit, her headaches disappeared and her husband softened toward the gospel.

When nursed instead of nipped, hurt feelings may carry a high price tag, such as indigestion, insomnia, fatigue, and carelessness issuing in accidents. What we eat may not harm us as much as what may be eating us.

To prevent resentment from growing into sulky self-pity or vengeful spite, Christ instructed His followers to air their grievances immediately. Though righteous in-

You Don't Have to Go It Alone

dignation is not forbidden, we should keep short accounts. Paul says, "Be ye angry, and sin not: let not the sun go down upon your wrath" (Ephesians 4:26). If a quarrel develops at the supper table, and the sun sets at 8:00 p.m., we have just two hours to settle the situation. How sad the story of the father, who, hearing his son had just been seriously injured in a motorcycle accident, moaned, "I wouldn't speak to him when he left. We had an argument."

Unless checked early, an unforgiving spirit can persist like a lingering illness. A male teacher who, in the shuffle of changing Bible study classes in an adult Sunday School no longer had a class, gradually dropped out of the department. When the man who had been appointed teacher in his place paid a visit to the displaced, disgruntled absentee, the latter displayed great rancor, calling the visitor all sorts of names. It took four years before the man was willing to admit he had been nurturing this grudge.

A woman became seriously ill. Her husband related that one of the most pitiful scenes he had ever witnessed was that of a lady walking into his house to apologize to his sick wife. This lady had carried a grudge since the couples' wedding day twenty years before because the wife had not asked her friend to be her maid of honor.

How fruitless that she had harbored that ill will in the first place, let alone carried it for all those years. The author of Hebrews wrote, ". . . lest any root of bitterness springing up trouble you, and thereby many be defiled" (Hebrews 12:15).

Corrie ten Boom relates how, upon meeting a lady in Germany who would not look at her directly, Corrie recognized her as the nurse who had been so cruel to her sister, Betsie, in a World War II concentration camp. The nurse had never asked forgiveness of Corrie ten Boom. At the moment of recognition, Corrie felt hatred in her heart.

Recognizing the wrong and not wishing resentment to get a stronghold within, she prayed, "O Lord, I'm not able to forgive, but thank You that You have brought into my heart God's love through the Holy Spirit which has been given me. Thank You that Your love in me is stronger than my bitterness and hatred."

Then Corrie went to the nurse and shook hands with her, even before the nurse could ask forgiveness.

Abstain from revenge. Not only should we refrain from returning evil for evil, but we should be prepared to do the evildoer good, as if he had not done us any wrong. Does not God make His sun shine on the evil and His rain fall on the unjust also? We are commanded to love our enemies, do good to those hating us, and pray for those despitefully using and persecuting us.

A lady's plump chicken was killed by her neighbor's dog. The neighbor deliberately let his animal run unchecked. The lady baked the chicken and sent it along with tasty trimmings to her neighbor. The gesture, bathed in the aroma of a delicious dish, broke down the mean-tempered neighbor, who came over to apologize profusely and genuinely.

Even though insulted by a mother whose daughter wanted the lead part in the church play, a youth advisor did not spite the mother by withholding the cherished part from her daughter, but gave it to her as though nothing had happened.

D. L. Moody once said, "I can imagine Jesus saying, 'Go search out the man who put the crown of thorns on My brow; tell him I will have a crown for him in My kingdom if he will accept salvation; and there shall not be a thorn in it.

" 'Find that man who smote the reed on My head, driving the thorns deeper into My brow. Tell him I want to give him a scepter.

" 'Go seek out that poor soldier who drove the spear into My side; tell him that there is a nearer way to My heart than that!' "

Have the spirit of forgiveness. Abandoned by her husband of many years for another woman, the wife made vain attempts to rebuild the original relationship singlehandedly and was repeatedly rejected. By her persistence, she was punishing herself unnecessarily. Though she rightfully hoped for a change, the dashing of that hope over and over again brought her more pain than God would expect this Christian woman to bear. God wished her to be ready to forgive, but she could not forgive her ex-husband if he did not want to be forgiven. Even God does not do that. What we need to have is the *spirit* or *willingness* to forgive.

Though we are to have the readiness to forgive, we cannot actually forgive someone who isn't asking for forgiveness. Only when a person genuinely repents can we forgive. When his change of heart is of unquestioned sincerity, then we can restore him to our confidence. Jesus said, ". . . If thy brother trespass against thee, rebuke him; and if he repent, forgive him" (Luke 17:3). If he repent.

Jesus' prayer for forgiveness at His crucifixion is not always understood. This prayer was not a wholesale request for pardon for everyone at the cross. Such a petition would have been inconsistent with divine holiness and human freedom. Pardon is never thrust on anyone; it comes through the channel of faith. The sin which caused Jesus' death could not be ignored. His prayer, "Father, forgive them, for they know not what they do," did not ask for cancellation of the condemnation, but for abeyance of the consequences until they understood to some degree the heinousness of their actions. Later, in a sermon to the people, Peter preached, "I wot that through ignorance ye did it" (Acts 3:17).

If Christ's prayer had not been uttered, immediate doom would likely have struck those that clamored for His execution. But Jesus prayed, in effect, "Hold the lightning back for now. Some will turn to Me when the significance of their crime dawns on them. Father, postpone the day of doom. Give them opportunity to believe on Me."

Because of this prayer, the dying thief was saved (Luke 23:39-43); perhaps the centurion (Matthew 27:54); three thousand people fifty days later (Acts 2:38-41); and a great company of priests a few months after (Acts 6:7). But not everyone at the cross received forgiveness. Even though Jesus delayed the doom of Jerusalem forty years from the time He wept over it, judgment came in A.D. 70.

A young man who had absconded with money from his mother in England emigrated to Canada. Years later the remorseful son told a preacher his story, ending, "I want to find my mother so that I may pay back the money I stole from her."

The preacher asked some minister friends in England to trace the mother. Back came a letter from a London pastor, "I finally tracked her down but one week too late. I was told her very last words were a prayer for her lost boy, charging a relative at her bedside, 'If ever you find my boy, tell him that his mother died forgiving him, and ask him to ask forgiveness from Jesus.' "

Though the son was only now asking the pardon, his

mother had the willingness to forgive long years before he was actually forgiven.

Jesus said, "And when ye stand praying, forgive, if ye have ought against any" (Mark 11:25). He warned, in effect, that uncharitable, resentful feelings would short-circuit spiritual power. Therefore, even before we forgive, we must harbor no bitterness, abstain from revenge, seek to return good for evil, and have the spirit of forgiveness.

AT THE POINT OF FORGIVENESS

Though forgiveness cannot be granted until the offender asks for it, when requested it should be granted in the spirit in which Christ forgave us—immediately and fully.

First, forgive immediately. To pout and sulk while doling out a hesitant forgiveness is neither helpful nor healthy for it saps spiritual vitality. Jesus always forgave immediately. He painted a verbal picture of this precept in the parable of the prodigal son whose loving father, as soon as the penitent boy blurted out, "I've sinned," asked for the fatted calf, the ring, the best robe and a homecoming party (Luke 15:11-24).

To the man sick with palsy, Jesus uttered cheering words at once: "Thy sins be forgiven thee" (Matthew 9:2). He instantly absolved the woman taken in adultery: "Neither do I condemn thee; go, and sin no more" (John 8:11b). He promptly forgave Zacchaeus his greed for gold and fraudulent practices, saying, "This day is salvation come to this house" (Luke 19:9b). To the repentant thief pardon was pronto: "Today shalt thou be with me in paradise" (Luke 23:43).

A prior spirit of forgiveness will make it easier to

forgive an offender. Interestingly, of the seven last say-ings Christ uttered, the only one He repeated over and over was His prayer for forgiveness for His tormentors as He was being crucified.

Perhaps with each blow of the nails through His hands and feet He kept saying, "Father forgive them. Father forgive them. Forgive them . . . ." Because of His magnanimous attitude He was able to forgive immediate-ly the dying thief, the 3,000, then a great company of priests, persecutor Saul, and all who asked for mercy— every case without delay of pardon.

An ancient monastic custom called for the brothers to beg and grant forgiveness of each other as part of every evening's devotions, so no rancor would be carried over to the next day.

Second, forgive fully. A lady said to her pastor, "I'll forgive Mrs. X, but I won't have anything to do with her. I don't wish to see her again. I won't let her in my house!"

The pastor replied, "Suppose Christ treats you the same way. He won't have anything to do with you from here on in. He won't let you into His presence. Or welcome you into His heavenly home some day!"

Imposing some condition, whether explicit or implicit, on an offender reveals imperfect, and incomplete pardon. David's halfhearted forgiveness of Absalom led to later rebellion by his son (II Samuel 14:24).

To forgive as Christ forgives is to give complete accep-tance to the culprit. Typical of Christ, Joseph totally forgave his brothers for their crime of selling him into slavery despite their needless worry that his pardon was only valid as long as their father lived (Genesis 50:1-21).

Forgiveness and forgiving are really two sides of the same coin. Christ's forgiveness should make us willing to

67

forgive others. The person who refuses to fully forgive others may be revealing that he has not fully experienced the forgiveness of Christ. The only section of the Lord's prayer which Jesus elaborated on was the clause on forgiveness. Immediately after the "amen," Jesus commented, "For if ye forgive men their trespasses, your heavenly Father will also forgive you: But if ye forgive not men their trespasses, neither will your Father forgive your trespasses" (Matthew 6:14,15).

In the parable of the merciless servant, Jesus used exaggeration to teach the indispensability of a forgiving spirit. A servant who owed his master a staggering debt of roughly seventeen million dollars begged for mercy. Sometime after receiving it, he refused a plea for mercy from a fellow servant who owed him a debt of around $17.00. Upon hearing of the servant's lack of compassion, the master tossed the unforgiving servant into prison.

Jesus ended the story, "So likewise shall my heavenly Father do also unto you, if ye from your hearts forgive not every one his brother their trespasses" (Matthew 18:35).

Our trespasses against Christ are mountainous compared to wrongs fellow believers do against us. Refusal to forgive another indicates failure to realize the enormity of our debt to Christ and of the vastness of His grace and mercy extended to us. An unforgiving spirit betrays an unforgiven spirit. He who is forgiven much should love much.

AFTER FORGIVENESS

Forgiveness which is patterned after Christ's forgiveness will not throw a confessed wrong back into an offender's face. Moreover, if another instance of pardon for the same incident is later requested, it should be granted—and granted repeatedly.

Forgive finally. How often people react, "I'll forgive, but I won't forget." To nurse a grievance indicates a lack of full and final forgiveness on the part of the forgiver. If we forgive completely we will also forget. The Lord has promised to remember our sin no more.

In a dream a man sinned and confessed it to the Lord. Ten minutes later he committed the same sin and muttered, "Oh, God, there I went and did it again." A big booming voice came out of the clouds, "Did what?"

The Corinthian church, at first lax in discipline, apparently swung to the other extreme and was having a hard time fully forgiving an immoral member.

Paul wrote to them, saying, "Sufficient to such a man is this punishment, which was inflicted of many. So that contrariwise ye ought rather to forgive him, and comfort him, lest perhaps such a one should be swallowed up with overmuch sorrow. Wherefore I beseech you that ye would confirm your love toward him" (II Corinthians 2:6,7).

To forget doesn't mean we won't remember. Our past is part of us; it cannot be obliterated, but, though the injury may be recalled, the old hurt is not relived over and over again, to be reviewed and resuffered. The sting of the wound has healed.

Genuine forgiveness welds severed friendships into a stronger reunion. The altercation is unalterable history, but its significance has changed; it has diminished. Our reaction to an incident matters much more than the incident itself.

A mother told her four-year-old daughter to stop jumping on the couch, especially since Mother's favorite lamp stood on the table next to the couch. A family

69

heirloom, the lamp was always glowing when guests were scheduled to arrive.

From the kitchen a few minutes later, Mother heard sounds of her little girl jumping on the couch followed by a crash. After spanking the little girl, Mother held her in her arms and told her why she had been punished—for bouncing on the couch when she had been told not to. Then, gathering the fragments of the broken lamp, she added, "As far as the lamp is concerned, Mommy forgives you and will never mention it to you again, ever."

The next day Mother accidentally stepped on one of her little girl's toys and smashed it to pieces. Mother felt awful, but the little girl ran over, picked up the pieces and said, "Mommy, I forgive you for that, and I'll never mention it to you again, ever."

It has been said that Abraham Lincoln's heart was so big it had no room for the memory of a wrong. Corrie ten Boom reminds us that when God casts someone's sins into the depths of the sea, He figuratively places a sign nearby, "No Fishing."

Forgive repeatedly. A man retorted, "I'll forgive him this time, but never again." What if Christ said the same to us?

Christ taught that forgiveness should be magnanimous and repeated. Peter once asked, ". . . Lord, how oft shall my brother sin against me, and I forgive him? till seven times?" (Matthew 18:21).

We feel a kinship with Peter in his down-to-earth question. After we have forgiven a person who then repeats the same or a greater wrong and again asks pardon, we wonder how long we are bound to let the process go on. Peter generously suggested the limit of seven times, a number far in excess of rabbinical teaching which decreed three times.

He scarcely could have anticipated the celestial arithmetic of forgiveness contained in Jesus' answer, "Until seventy times seven" (Verse 22). Even if the number is 77, as suggested by a marginal note in the Revised Standard Version, the figure is staggering, removing all boundaries to repetition of forgiveness.

When someone doesn't listen to our instructions carefully on the initial giving, we scold, "Listen this time, for I won't repeat it." When we say, "I'll overlook it this once, but don't let it happen again," we virtually declare our unwillingness to forgive more than once. But Jesus once commanded the disciples to forgive the same person seven times in the same day, if he repented (Luke 17:4).

"Of course," notes commentator John A. Broadus in *Commentary on the Gospel of Matthew,* "All this rests on the supposition that we believe the man sincerely repents. Otherwise we are not bound to forgive even once, in the full sense of restoring to confidence and affection."[10]

A widow had a heart full of hate for a man who had been a business competitor of her late husband. Left with four children and no insurance or money, she hung on to his electrical supply company, depending almost entirely on the help of the man her husband had trained for six years. Her husband's lone competitor in the community tried to buy her out at only a fraction of what the business was worth. When she refused, he angrily tried to force her out by cutting prices and doing all he could to hurt her. But she hung on.

The last straw came when her right-hand, husband-trained man defected to her competitor because he offered more salary than she could pay. She struggled on as best she could, but often the family didn't have enough to

71

You Don't Have to Go It Alone

eat. Hatred poisoned her soul.

One night, as she went to church, the sermon dealt with the sufferings of Christ. The preacher asked the congregation to imagine they were traveling back across the years watching Christ pray in Gethsemane, sweating great drops of blood. He described the coming of the soldiers to arrest Him, Judas' betrayal with a kiss, His trials before Annas, Herod and Pilate.

The preacher described how the soldiers stripped off Jesus' clothes, covered Him with mock royalty, spat on Him, struck Him, drove nails through His hands and feet. Then the preacher spoke of the mockery by the leaders, by the mob, even by the thieves on either side of the cross.

For forty-five minutes the pastor described the wicked behavior against the lovely, sinless, spotless Son of God as vividly as he could. Then after a pause, he said, "Listen, Jesus is about to speak. We strain our ears. And across the centuries His voice comes clear and firm, 'Father, forgive them.' "

When the preacher invited people to come to the altar to pray, this lady said, "I could think only of that competitor I hated. I found myself praying for him. I prayed the prayer Jesus had prayed. I felt cleansed and forgiven. Now I have no fear of the future for my family and me. And I hold no grudge against that man."

A general once said to John Wesley, "I never forgive." Came Wesley's reply, "Then, I hope, sir, that you never sin."

6
Forbearing One Another

An old preacher used to say that the secret of a happy marriage was "five bears—bear and forbear." The Apostle Paul urged believers to forbear one another (Ephesians 4:2; Colossians 3:13). Opportunities to exercise forbearance surround us, and we are called upon to manifest it in all areas of life.

Certain temptations, of course, rarely, if ever, confront us. How many believers would give a moment's contemplation to robbing a bank, hijacking a plane, or murdering someone? But the numerous and often close relationships at home, office, school, factory, church, all provide frequent, if not almost continuous situations that require forbearance.

This virtue is needed to face the countless frustrations stemming from the ordinary course of events, such as someone butting ahead of us in line at a counter, getting caught behind a stalled car in a traffic jam, or being delayed in a doctor's office. One preacher said, "We get mad if we miss one section of a revolving door, whereas our grandparents didn't get irritated if they missed the stagecoach for they knew another one would be along the next month." Someone commented, "There would be fewer pedestrian patients if there were more patient pedestrians."

Family living especially provides many an irritant. Someone takes too long to comb her hair. Another plays the radio too loudly. Still another squeezes the toothpaste from the middle or doesn't hang his towel straight, or fails to wash the ring out of the bathtub, or dries shirts in the shower, or suffers the jibes of a non-believing mate. Even Christian husbands and wives need forbearance.

The late Dr. Harry Ironside, well-known Bible teacher, told how he reprimanded his wife rather sharply late one Sunday night. "You should not have spoken so abruptly to me. Do you realize I preached six times today?" She replied, "Do you realize I had to listen to you six times today?"

The need for forbearance showed up in a man's devotions when he prayed, "Dear Lord, please send me patience, but send it immediately."

Because of its almost continuous and ubiquitous need, the command to be forbearing is so vital.

WHAT IS FORBEARANCE?

The root meaning of the two words that combine to give us "forbear" is *holding back*. "Forbear" means to endure, bear with, suffer, permit, put up with. After the Transfiguration, when the disciples could not cure a demon-possessed boy, Jesus asked, "How long shall I suffer you?" He was asking, "How long shall I keep on putting up with your unbelief?"

Forbear has been translated "to have patience one with another." More than once forbearing is linked to long-suffering (Ephesians 4:2; Colossians 3:12-13). It involves reasonableness, gentleness, suppression of anger, slowness to resentment, endurance of the weaknesses of others. Forbearance creates in us a disposition to take wrong rather than stand upon the last jot of our rights. We are slow to take offense, are not irascible, do not flare up at the least provocation, favor a return of good for evil. Forbearance is a precondition of forgiveness.

High in the Andes Mountains when pack goats meet each other on a narrow ledge where passing is impossible, one goat will often kneel and let the other walk over him, to the safety of both. Occasions come when, for the best of all, we should kneel and let a person walk over us.

Forbearance is a fruit of the Spirit, certainly more desirable than ostentatious gifts. In the judgment of heaven, the mother who bears a difficult family situation hour after hour, day after day, is far more spiritual than the flamboyant, exhibitionist, self-seeking preacher.

A Christian foreman was the constant butt of sneering remarks by an abusive workman. Instead of reprimanding the youthful employee, the foreman took the insults so gracefully that people admired his patience.

He explained, "Up our way there's a dog which, whenever the moon is full, goes out and sits and barks for hours at night."

When he said no more, a questioner would invariably ask, "What about the dog and the moon?" Smiling, the foreman would reply, "The moon doesn't pay any attention. It just keeps right on shining."

75

You Don't Have to Go It Alone

Forbearance is the grace to keep on shining for the Lord amid the pack of barking dogs.

When we resent a wrong done to us by another, three reactions are possible, two of which are not healthy. Losing our temper is damaging. But the other extreme, silently nursing our grudge, directs poison inward to fester in our spiritual system. The healthy, Christian reaction is to state our grievance calmly and forthrightly to the one wronging us (Matthew 18:15-17). Of course, none of these reactions would be necessary if we could find it in ourselves to overlook a potential wrong.

The Bible contains several instances of forbearance. When Isaac successfully dug a well only to have it appropriated by neighboring herdsmen, he moved to another location and dug again. When neighbors claimed a second well, he again exercised forbearance. When he found a third well they left him alone (Genesis 26:17-22).

How longsuffering was David when hounded by King Saul. Twice he could have killed Saul but did not take matters into his own hands (I Samuel 24:7; I Samuel 26:22-23). Nehemiah remained patient in the face of mockings by Sanballat during the rebuilding of the walls of Jerusalem (Nehemiah 4:1). The patience of Job is proverbial (Book of Job). Stephen displayed the virtue of forbearance in the face of violent death (Acts 7:55-60). When Paul testified of his own longsuffering, anyone reading a list of his privations would readily agree that he displayed forbearance (II Corinthians 6:6; II Timothy 3:10; II Corinthians 11:23-27).

But of course the supreme example of forbearance was the Lord Jesus Christ. To His disciples who repeatedly argued even up to the night before He died as to who would be top man in the kingdom, He exercised longsuffering, teaching over and over the lesson of humility.

For those persistently plotting against Him, He reserved His invectives until the last week of His life. About to be betrayed, denied and forsaken, He prayed in the Garden for those who would be unfaithful. After His disciples had fallen asleep three times, despite His express request for them to watch and pray, without recrimination (though with mild rebuke) He then watched over the drowsy disciples.

He was painstakingly patient to Judas in the moment of betrayal, even permitting the betrayer to besmirch His holy cheek with a mock kiss. How forbearing to Malchus whose ear He restored, even though he was among the mob in the Garden arresting Him. How forbearing on the cross!

VALUE OF FORBEARANCE

Forbearance strengthens control of self, and leads to added maturity. Lack of self-control packs dangerous potential. A lady said, "I've a bad temper, but it's over in a moment." Came the reply, "So is a shotgun blast—but it blows everything to bits!"

An unknown poet has written:

> When I have lost my temper I have lost my
>   reason too,
> I'm never proud of anything which angrily I
>   do.
> When I have talked in anger and my cheeks
>   were flaming red,
> I have always uttered something which I
>   wish I hadn't said.
> In anger I have never done a kindly deed
>   or wise,
> But many things for which I felt I should

> apologize.
> In looking back across my life, and all I've
>   lost or made,
> I can't recall a single time when fury ever
>   paid.
> So I struggle to be patient, for I've reached
>   a wiser age;
> I do not want to do a thing or speak a word
>   in rage.
> I have learned by sad experience that when
>   my temper flies
> I never do a worthy thing, a decent deed or
>   wise.

The proverb puts it, "He that is slow to anger is better than the mighty; and he that ruleth his spirit than he that taketh a city" (Proverbs 16:32).

Irritations productively handled help us grow. Tribulation creates patience in us, and patience develops maturity. James wrote, ". . . that the trying of your faith worketh patience. But let patience have her perfect work, that ye may be perfect and entire, wanting nothing" (James 1:3-4). Pressure brings patience, which in turn brings perfection (maturity).

Forbearance helps maintain peace with others. If we can delay our unkind reaction to an unkind action against us by another, we give the offender time to reflect on his deed and to perhaps express regret or apology. Thus, forbearance helps create peace through understanding on our part and reflection by the other.

When a man was awakened just after midnight by a neighbor who was clipping his hedge with an electric trimmer, the man's first reaction was to blow his top. But after pausing momentarily he pursued another approach.

Still clad in pajamas, he grabbed his own hedge clipper

and joined his neighbor, offering to help. The neighbor, taken somewhat aback, gladly accepted the offer, acknowledged it as a real neighborly act, and at the same time stammered out some sort of apology.

"Think nothing of it," came the reply. "I figured that by helping you it would take half as long and I could get back to sleep that much sooner."

A man who was repeatedly irritated with his neighbors built a cement block fence around his yard at much expense, thinking he had shut out the nosy, noisy neighbors.

How different that was from two neighbors on the next street who had no high fence between their properties, but rather a six-foot strip of unusually rich, green grass, much more luxuriant than the lawns on either side.

When asked to explain, they laughed. One explained, "We're so afraid we'll cheat each other that we always fertilize about three feet across our property line on the other fellow's side. And we water the grass the same way, so that six-foot strip on our property line gets double the fertilizer and water of our own yards." Forbearance smooths the "sandpaper" between people.

Michael R. Tucker offers the testimony of members of a growing church in Colorado in *The Church That Dared To Change:*

" . . . No one gets his first choice all the time. Sure, we've had disagreements about the color of new carpet, removal of a wall, singing of certain songs, use of the buildings, choice of words, order of services, and multitudes of other matters. But still we don't fight, pout or disrupt God's work. Emotionally mature people and groups make decisions in an orderly way. Willingness to compromise is part of Christian maturity. Compromise must be done with a smile, realizing that partial ac-

79

complishment is better than none."[11]

An older woman, a long-time member of a church, came to her pastor declaring that she was upset about the church opening a coffeehouse to reach the counter-culture. She expressed firm opposition, then finished by saying, "Pastor, here's five dollars for that ministry."

Frequently we must bend a little in order to oil the friction of personal interaction.

Forbearance opens our eyes to the needs of others. By failing to forbear, we blind ourselves to the problems of others. Thus, we deprive ourselves of opportunities for service.

If someone becomes irritated or upset, instead of following suit we would be wise to pause to try to discover the reason for the other's disturbed condition. Perhaps one has a sick child, has lost his job, is ill. Or maybe we expect too much of a new Christian, or too much success from missionaries in difficult places.

Ian Maclaren wrote, "Let us be kind to one another, for most of us are fighting a hard battle." Someone commented, "This would make an excellent motto on a business desk or a bedroom bureau. We are fully aware of our own struggles but are often blind to the battles others have to fight."

Forbearance displays the reality of our profession. A man in a suburb north of New York City taught a Bible class for teenagers. One day his phone rang, and a voice said, "What have you done to my daughter?" The teacher thought he was in for a tongue-lashing from the father until the conversation continued. "She used to have a violent temper. Now she hardly ever loses it. What did you do to her?"

The teacher answered, "The Lord did it."

A man recording a gospel song had to repeat it thirteen

times because the engineer kept muffing the machine. The soloist said, "Let's pray." They prayed. Something went wrong with the equipment on the next try. They prayed again. Then on the fifteenth attempt the recording went smoothly. The engineer marveled at the Christian soloist's patience.

A phone operator said to the student of a Christian college, "The dean at your school is so gracious. I got him the wrong number three times in a row, and he never grumbled."

Paul thought it scandalous that members of the church at Corinth would take one another to law. He rebuked them: "Now therefore there is utterly a fault among you, because ye go to law one with another. Why do ye not rather take wrong? why do ye not rather suffer yourselves to be defrauded?" (I Corinthians 6:7). This lack of forbearance was especially serious because it was "before the unbelievers" (verse 6), thus bringing the Christian faith into disrepute.

Several young people were invited to watch a translation committee at work on the final version of Daniel. The scholars considered each verse separately, then each phrase in the verse, then they discussed the proper wording for the verse to be translated. Afterwards they voted, and the vote ended the discussion, for all bowed to the majority.

Later, a girl from that youth group rose in her church prayer meeting to report on her experience. She said, "Pastor, we saw men submitting one to another." The mutual forbearance of the translators had left an indelible mark.

A Latin American evangelist, impeccably dressed in a white summer suit, was sitting in a restaurant when a waiter spilled soup over his coat and trousers. Deeply em-

81

barrassed, the waiter apologized profusely. The evangelist graciously overlooked the incident. The next day when the evangelist entered the restaurant the waiter asked for a private appointment. The evangelist's unresentful treatment of the incident made the waiter inquire about the message the evangelist proclaimed.

WHAT MOTIVATES FORBEARANCE?

The command of the Father motivates forbearance. The biblical command to forbearance should be enough to make us resolve by divine grace to let longsuffering prevail in our lives. The God who commanded it put up with Noah's generation for perhaps 120 years.

The literal meaning of *slow to anger* is long of nose or long of breathing. How picturesque! As a person begins to lose his temper and anger begins to boil, one sign is often the dilating of the nostrils. A snorting, charging bull is an emblem of anger. But God is in no hurry to retaliate. He does not fly into a rage at the least provocation. He does not react quickly. He has self-restraint.

In dealing with Pharaoh, God was so patient. He also exhibited a pattern of longsuffering with Paul, this ringleader who with blood on his hands was a most unlikely candidate for conversion, a zealot who would travel dozens of miles to imprison those of the Way.

If God has exhibited "good and forbearance and long-suffering" toward us, should we not put up with a lot from others? (Romans 2:4).

The example of Christ motivates forbearance. Christ's most impressive exhibition of forbearance should motivate us to forbearance. In the face of derision, mockery, betrayal, insensitivity, denials, arrest, trials, scourging and crucifixion, He reviled not again (I Peter

2:18-23).

The fruit of the Spirit motivates forbearance. Love, the all-embracing fruit of the Spirit "suffereth long, and is kind . . . Beareth all things, believeth all things, hopeth all things, endureth all things" (I Corinthians 13:4-7). More specifically, longsuffering is the fourth listed fruit of the Spirit (Galatians 5:22).

Of major help in our effort to forbear is the realization of the impermanence of circumstances. Irritations and troubles which bother us today are temporary and will pass in God's good time. Because relief will come, we should trust in God who works all things out. The sufferings of this present time are not worthy to be compared with the glory that shall be revealed.

In the meantime, any lapses in the forbearance should cause us to seek forgiveness immediately. Dr. M. R. DeHaan is quoted in his biography as saying that he did not always treat his wife, Priscilla, like the queen he considered her to be. On one occasion the Holy Spirit convicted him through a meditation he himself had written. Arriving at the office one morning he told the story.

"This morning Mrs. DeHaan and I had a little disagreement, and I didn't say anything at all as we ate breakfast. Finally it was time to read the devotional in *Our Daily Bread*. She did so silently to herself for a moment. Then taking it and shoving it under my nose she asked, 'Are you the man who wrote this?' I read the article and felt about an inch tall. It had to do with kindness and forbearance. That did it. We had to make up right there. It's so easy to preach but so much more difficult to practice.''[12]

7
Ministering One to Another

A member of a church with 400 in regular attendance was asked by a friend, "How many ministers does your church have?"

His friend was jolted by the answer. "Four hundred, but only two get paid!"

Some folk may believe the church is a place for solace rather than for service, but the New Testament teaches that every believer is a minister. Peter wrote, "As every man hath received the gift, even so minister the same one to another, as good stewards of the manifold grace of God" (I Peter 4:10).

The entire Christian community is to be active in a ministry. This doctrine is called "the priesthood of believers," a principle which Martin Luther championed.

In effect, it implies the right and responsibility of every believer to read the Bible in his native tongue, to make private judgment thereon, to go directly to the throne of grace without any human mediator, and to participate actively in the work of the church according to his particular gift and calling.

Peter called all believers "an holy priesthood." As priests, we offer up spiritual sacrifices, good works, prayers and praises as well as our own bodies (Romans 12:1; Hebrews 13:15; I Peter 2:5). The office of priest raises all Christians to the status of "ministers." All saints should be known by one word: *servant.* Christ was the primary Minister or Servant, and continues His ministry through His ministers.

Too often the pastor is a prima donna, jack-of-all-trades, superstar, trying to do all the jobs in the church. Though the pastor does exercise priesthood, so do all Christians. The pastor's ministry is carried out, not instead of the people, but alongside them. If the gospel is to be preached, burdens borne, the unlearned taught, the perplexed counseled, people will have to join the pastor in serving for no man can do it by himself. Perhaps renewal will come only as the laity become ministers.

In a recent ten-year period in Brazil, large gains were made by several churches. Mission leaders attribute this unparalleled expansion to the high level of "people" participation. Church life should not be a spectator sport.

Modern man often can discern no purpose for living: he lacks a sense of worth and direction. He may feel like a cog in some big machine, or like a man whose press produces a part for a plane engine, but who doesn't know the purpose of that part.

When a group of workers who drilled holes six feet deep in a street were then told without any explanation to

85

fill them up, they announced to the boss that they were quitting. Their explanation: "Digging holes and filling them up again makes fools of us." When the boss enlightened them, "We're trying to find the location of a lost water main," they resumed their digging.

Down deep a human desires to see a rationale for what he does. The Christian should derive a sense of vocation from the truth that every believer is a minister with a job to do in the body of Christ. The practice of the biblical doctrine of the priesthood of believers taps reservoirs of spiritual manpower, releases frozen assets, reduces unemployment among saints and leads to the edification of the church.

BELIEVERS MINISTER THROUGH GIFTS

We are to minister to each other, "as every man hath received the gift." Every believer has a gift or gifts assigned to us at the moment of our regeneration. Though they may lie dormant for months, even years, they are given to us at our spiritual birthday. The word for gift, *charisma*, was employed by the Greeks to refer to a birthday gift.

Like Peter, Paul stressed the universality of gifts. "But unto every one of us is given grace according to the measure of the gift of Christ" (Ephesians 4:7). Without exception, every new believer—even if unschooled, fresh from heathenism, or of wicked background—is the recipient of a gift or gifts. The Apostle Paul, a violent, blaspheming persecutor of the church, received gifts the moment he was converted. The Corinthians boasted of gifts in abundance, though only a short time redeemed from flagrant wickedness (I Corinthians 1:7; 6:9-11).

If we are tempted to succumb to an inferiority complex, we should repeat, "I am a gifted child of God." Such an awareness should meet the psychological need of Christians to feel wanted and worthy. Believers can build each other's self image by pointing out positive strengths in one another.

Our spiritual gifts are given to us so that we can minister to others. They are to be exercised for the health of the whole body. In I Corinthians 12, Paul takes an entire chapter to expound this concept. Just as a human body has many parts which belong to that one body, it is so with Christ's body (verse 12). The various gifts are bestowed for the mutual profit of all believers.

In Christ, the interrelationships and mutual assistance are to be as cooperative and complementary as the various organs of the human body (I Corinthians 12:14-27). The eye cannot say it has no need of the ear. If all were hands, how would we walk? Each member of the body is needed to serve the whole. Our gifts are needed to strengthen other believers. In turn, we shall be helped toward maturity through others' gifts.

A fellow in Argentina, conscripted for military service, showed up at basic camp objecting, "What good am I? I have no arms!" The officer in charge pointed to a fellow pumping water. "Go tell him when the pail is full. He cannot see!"

Gifts are not for self-congratulatory prestige, nor for individual glory, nor for one's own personal spiritual benefit, but for the common good. Paul put it this way: "But the manifestation of the Spirit is given to every man to profit withal" (I Corinthians 12:7). "To profit withal" may be translated, "for the common good." Spiritual abilities are for the benefit of others, for the upbuilding of the church.

The Spirit gave gifts "for the perfecting of the saints,

for the work of the ministry, for the edifying of the body of Christ" (Ephesians 4:12). The two commas in the verse seem to say that gifts have three purposes. But to get the apostle's correct meaning, we should omit the commas: Gifts are for "the perfecting of the saints" so that they can do "the work of the ministry" so that such service will result in the "edifying of the body of Christ." Restating it, gifts prepare saints for the task of ministering in order to build up the body of Christ.

A wrong attitude laments, "Why should I attend church? I get nothing out of it." Attendance and involvement will enable us to minister through our gifts for the good of our fellow saints. In turn, others will contribute to our spiritual edification.

Whenever John Bunyan visited London, Dr. John Owen, scholarly Chancellor of Oxford University, used to go hear the unschooled mender of pots and pans preach. One day King Charles asked Owen why, with all his knowledge, he bothered to hear the simple tinker preach. Replied Owen, "Had I the tinker's gifts, I'd gladly surrender my learning."

The need for mutual ministry rules out the lone-wolf type of service. No individual believer is gifted enough, smart enough, or strong enough to live apart from others. The true significance of the Reformation phrase, "priesthood of believers," is not that everybody is his own priest, but rather that everybody must be a priest to somebody else. Everybody needs somebody.

EACH BELIEVER MINISTERS DIFFERENTLY

An orchestra has many kinds of instruments—string, percussion, wind—each with its distinctive sound, depending on the ability of the player. Even if one instru-

ment is played beautifully, the full richness of compositions can only be realized when the entire orchestra
blends together, with each musician playing his best on
his violin, flute, clarinet, or other instrument. Similarly,
as each Christian plays his instrument under the leadership and lordship of Christ, the church will make sym-
phony, not cacophony.

One night amidst the peal of the organ, the blare of
horns and clashing of cymbals, a piccolo player far back
in the orchestra thought his shrill note would not be
missed. Immediately the conductor flung up his hands to
halt the music. He knew someone had failed to play his
instrument. Every believer must exercise his individual
gift so that the whole body of Christ may function.

In reality, we are not born equal. Though we share the
same Holy Spirit who enables all believers to confess
Jesus as Lord (I Corinthians 12:3), and who has baptized
all believers into the body of Christ (verse 13), we receive
different spiritual gifts for service. This is why Paul uses
the analogy of the human body with its varied members—
eyes, ears, hands, feet, nose—to illustrate the diverse gifts
within the body of Christ.

How many different gifts are there? Some list as few as
nine; others in the range of fifteen to twenty-two; and
some others estimate more. No one knows for sure. (See
the author's book, *19 Gifts of the Spirit.*[13])

How many gifts are assigned to each believer? At least
one, and likely more than one. In Christ's parable of the
talents, only one of the three recipients had just one
talent. The other two each had more than one, a combination of seven between them. Multiple gifts can be observed in New Testament characters, like Deacon Philip
who had the gifts of wisdom, showing mercy, evangelism,
and perhaps others.

You Don't Have to Go It Alone

Why do we get the particular gifts we do, making us different from others? Because the Holy Spirit sovereignly assigns to each believer as He wills (I Corinthians 12:11; Ephesians 4:7). "God set the members every one of them in the body, as it hath pleased him" (I Corinthians 12:18).

Because divine choice dictates the differences in gifts, no one should boast of his gifts. Paul pointed out, "For who maketh thee to differ from another? and what hast thou that thou didst not receive? now if thou didst receive it, why dost thou glory, as if thou hadst not received it?" (I Corinthians 4:7).

Neither should we idolize nor become the devotee of any human leader out of admiration for his charisma. Leaders are mere fellow servants, gifted apart from merit by the Spirit for a particular ministry.

Rather than envy anyone else for his gifts, we should thank God for one's evangelistic ability and another's teaching proficiency. And we should be content with God's choice of gifts for us. Isn't discontent a form of rebellion at the way the Spirit runs the church?

A tale is told of four animals who decided to better themselves by attending school where the curriculum included flying, swimming, climbing, and running. A rabbit, an expert in running, spent so much time in the areas of his deficiencies—flying, swimming and climbing—that his running suffered. The squirrel, a superior climber, majored in the other subjects to the detriment of his climbing. The duck, rated "A" in swimming, dropped to a "C" because his teachers spent days trying to teach him to climb, fly and run. The eagle for whom flying was natural looked pathetic climbing to the top of a tree.

Too often in the Lord's work we fail to accept our spiritual species and try to serve in areas for which we have not been gifted. We need to cultivate our own capabilities.

> Be not always wanting
> Some other work to do,
> But cheerfully perform the task
> Which Christ has set for you.
> —*Anonymous*

Joan and Betty, close Christian friends, each tried her hand at both entertaining and teaching home Bible classes. Joan had a miserable time with the entertainment part, and Betty with the teaching segment. But when they joined together, with Betty providing the hospitality and Joan leading the study, they were an unbeatable combination.

SOME WAYS WE MAY MINISTER TO EACH OTHER

The gift of prophecy, which ranks high in the lists of gifts (Romans 12:6; I Corinthians 12:28), is the Spirit-given ability to proclaim the written Word of God with clarity. Since it is so important, it should be prevalent. Probably it is possessed by far more saints than realize it. Some may have the ability to give forth the Word of God to adults. Others may be able to explain it to children, or in a small company of two or three, or to individuals. The gift may be used via proclamation over radio or television, or in neighborhood Bible classes or small groups. Many minister to fellow saints through propounding the Word.

We may serve other believers through the gift of shepherding. Norman, a high school senior who had fallen

You Don't Have to Go It Alone

head-over-heels for a fine Christian girl, a junior in high school, quietly announced their intent to marry after four months of acquaintance. A youth leader Norman respected pointed out to the senior that he had no job, that his girlfriend had another year of high school, that far too little time had elapsed for them to know each other well enough for marriage, and that the Bible presents a high view of marriage which requires much consideration before entering that holy estate. The youth leader was able to shepherd Norman from his rash course.

Great opportunities to minister to each other abound through the gift of teaching, the supernatural ability to explain clearly and apply effectively the truth of the Word of God. Some have the gift of teaching children, making an impact on successive waves of youngsters who pass through their classes in the early classes of Sunday school. Others relate well with teenagers.

Still others communicate best with the college crowd. Some share best with adults, others on a seminary level. Some travel as Bible teachers to large congregations and Bible conferences. Others lead small groups or disciple on a one-to-one basis. Paul exhorted women to be "teachers of good things" to children and younger women (Titus 2:3; II Timothy 1:5; 3:14,15).

How needed is the ministry of encouragement! A summer intern to high school youth came in tears to the Christian education director after a difficult youth meeting, ready to resign just two weeks into July. The director listened sympathetically, then pointed out how lives had already been changed through the intern's leadership. After adding a couple of suggestions to improve the youth group and prayer, the summer intern went back to his task with new resolve. Not only did he complete the summer successfully, but he later became a capable Christian education director in a large church.

Barnabas, of course, is our supreme biblical example in the ministry of encouragement. He was always so encouraging that fellow believers changed his name from Joses to Barnabas, meaning "son of encouragement" (Acts 4:36).

The gift of helps serves the church in a supporting, usually temporal role by releasing other workers to do their spiritual ministries. Paul and Barnabas had John Mark as their helper on their first missionary journey. He probably performed many menial jobs which freed them to better carry on their evangelistic and edifying endeavors. Paul always gathered about him a team of workers without whom he could not have possibly carried on his great ministry. Beloved Physician Luke must have been an invaluable assistant, especially during times of illness, beatings, stonings and other privations.

Some modern illustrations of helps include office work in a Christian organization, delivery of church flowers to the sick after Sunday services, taping of Christian broadcasts, driving the pastor to the airport, meeting a speaker at the station, preparing handwork for Vacation Bible School, and cooking meals for God's servants.

The gift of hospitality is the Spirit-given ability to provide open house and warm welcome to those in need of food and lodging. Itinerant preachers and traveling Christian business people in the early Christian church had no Howard Johnson's to feed and house them. Ancient inns were often brothels. Robbers and dangers threatened travelers, so Christians were exhorted to exercise hospitality and to open their homes to believing strangers (Romans 12:13; I Timothy 3:2; Titus 1:8; Hebrews 13:2; I Peter 4:9).

93

You Don't Have to Go It Alone

Though today, visiting Christian workers are often housed in motels, many families with extra bedrooms or apartments take delight in entertaining guest evangelists, Bible teachers, missionaries and touring Christian school choirs.

We can minister to others through the gift of giving. God gives the ability to make money to some men because He can trust them to use their assets for His glory. These men are special stewards, giving freely and joyfully. James Young, a chemist who devised a method of extracting oil from shale in the early 1850s, used his profits to help finance the missionary work and explorations of his boyhood friend, Dr. David Livingstone.

One pastor told of men with money who often approach him about some worthwhile local church ministry which needs financial support. They derive delight at seeing God work through their money, often at considerable cost to themselves. But the gift of giving is not confined to the rich. The Philippian church, which evidenced this grace by its repeated and warm financial help to the Apostle Paul, probably had members of minimal means. How often today people with little income give generously to every worthy cause their church undertakes.

The gift of mercy is needed to show practical, compassionate, bright love toward suffering members of Christ's body. A terminally ill man was dozing when a visitor walked in, laughing gayly with his greeting, "Hello, John! I've come to see you." A smile broke across the face of the patient who was suffering much. The visitor put his arm under the pillow and cradled the dying man in his embrace. His words flowed with praise to God—how wonderful He is, how He never makes a mistake, how marvelous it would be to see the Lord Jesus Christ.

Another person in the room commented, "That day I

saw the gift of showing mercy demonstrated through the ministry of this hospital visitor; he was empowered to speak with kindness and cheerfulness.''

RESPONSIBILITY FOR OUR GIFTS

We shall be held responsible for the use of our gifts, regardless of the number. It behooves us to discover, develop and deploy them. In the day of judgment we shall not be praised for magnificence of mansion, or for size of salary, or for farness of fame. But we shall hear, "Well done," if we have faithfully used the gifts divinely loaned us.

Some years ago typesetters for the *Times* of London failed to produce a copy free from typographical errors. The editors thought long and hard about how to correct the situation. They announced that the first copy of every edition would be sent free to their majesties, the king and queen. Immediately the errors dropped to virtually zero. Every child of the kingdom should administer his gift or gifts as unto the King of kings, and Lord of lords.

8
Building Up
One Another

The human body repairs itself. Not only is healthy tissue replaced, but injured cells are restored. The body has marvelous recuperative and corrective powers. Similarly, members of the body of Christ are urged to build each other up and to restore fallen brethren.

Though the topics considered in other chapters contribute to mutual upbuilding, like bearing others' burdens, confessing, forgiving, forbearing and ministering through spiritual gifts, perhaps the areas handled in this chapter contribute more directly to brotherly edification.

Paul wrote to the Colossians, "Let the word of Christ dwell in you richly in all wisdom; teaching and admonishing one another in psalms, hymns and spiritual songs, singing with grace in your hearts to the Lord"

(Colossians 3:16).

TEACHING

We are to teach each other the Word of God so that it may dwell in us richly. Who is to do the teaching? Every saint is to teach, for the command is to the entire church. Though New Testament leaders like Paul surrounded themselves with younger men who in turn trained others, the author of Hebrews implies that every believer should be engaged in the ministry of teaching. He reproves his readers by saying that by the time they should have grown sufficiently to instruct others, they themselves were still in need of someone teaching them the ABCs of the faith.

His exact words, "Ye ought to be teachers . . ." (Hebrews 5:12), indicate that every believer is obligated in his own way to be able to instruct others in biblical truth, even if he doesn't possess the gift of teaching. The rapid maturation of some Christians may be due to fresh insights into Scripture shared informally in small groups, as well as to formal pulpit instruction.

Before we can teach we must first have been equipped through someone else's teaching. Opportunities to learn should be faithfully explored. We can all learn something new from sermons, special meetings, Bible conferences, evening Bible schools, Bible study groups, and books explaining the Scripture.

Paul mentions music as a definite method of teaching each other, specifically by "psalms, hymns and spiritual songs." The psalms sung by early Christians still constitute a lovely part of Christian worship. Since the heathen commonly composed odes to false gods, it was natural for Christians to introduce songs of praise to their one true God. Soon, songs relating to spiritual matters

You Don't Have to Go It Alone

were composed. Precisely how the early church sang may be in doubt, but we are certain that sing they did—not only for worship but for teaching, too.

Through the centuries, godly music has contributed to the support of the Christian faith. The hymns of the Reformers helped spread their doctrine. Luther and Calvin both composed hymns, using the vernacular of the people and clothing the message in the familiar tunes of the day. Thus Reformation teaching sang its way into the hearts and homes of the commoners.

Dr. Ben Johnson once said that if he were allowed to make the ballads of a nation, he cared not who made the laws. The words of our church music are vitally important.

Two indispensable criteria for music performed by choirs and individuals is that the words be loyal to Scripture, and that they be understandable. If not intelligible, there will be no teaching. If not Scriptural, no word of Christ will be communicated. Tempo, melody and rhythm are relative factors in musical expression which are subordinate to the purpose of edification.

It's an all too prevalent habit for us to sing words without realizing what we are singing. When we concentrate on the catchy or familiar tune and pay no attention whatever to the message of the words, we do not teach ourselves. Too often at the end of a congregational song, few people have any idea of the message in the words. We need to sing together thoughtfully in order to build up one another.

We need to listen thoughtfully, also, to the words of choirs, quartets, trios, duets, and solos, which are sung for us. Performers need to bathe every special number in the prayer that God will use their voices to teach their hearers. Choir directors and singers should select

numbers that are imbued with sound evangelical senti-
ment in order to more effectively preserve and propagate
biblical truths.

Howard Rutledge tells how he struggled to recall Scriptures and hymns during the seven years he was a prisoner
in Vietnam. He wrote in his book, *In the Presence of
Mine Enemies:*

"I had spent my first eighteen years in a Southern Baptist Sunday school and I was amazed at how much I could
recall; regrettably I had not seen then the importance of
memorizing verses from the Bible or learning gospel
songs. I never dreamed that . . . thinking about one
memorized verse could have made a whole day bearable.
One portion of a verse I did remember was, 'Thy Word
have I hid in my heart.'

"Every day I planned to accomplish certain tasks. I
woke early, did my physical exercises, cleaned up as best I
could, then began a period of devotional prayer and
meditation. I would pray, hum silently, quote Scripture,
and think about what the verses meant to me."[14]

A Christian worker grew spiritually through a rebuke
he received as a boy, working in a store. Someone had
given him a book of pornographic cartoons, and when a
Christian businessman entered, the boy showed him a
page, thinking he would be amused. The moment the
mature believer comprehended the cartoon, he exclaimed
gently but firmly, "I'm disappointed in you. You've professed faith in Christ, yet somehow think these pictures
are funny. Filling your mind with these thoughts can only
harm you. Throw the book out and ask the Lord's
forgiveness."

The Christian worker still vividly recalls the shame and
resentment. Even though inclined at first to make some
excuse, he knew the man was right. He admitted his folly,

You Don't Have to Go It Alone

confessed to the Lord, and never forgot the admonition.

Admonishing is difficult, and a rapidly disappearing Christian service. Can you remember when you were last rebuked? Can you recall when you last admonished a friend? In reality, admonishment is inevitable, for when believers rub shoulders together, some crisis is bound to come when one person will find it necessary to confront another with God's Word and will.

Admonishing is more than teaching. Teaching is telling a person what to do. Admonishing is telling him what to do when he's done what he was told not to do. To admonish is to confront verbally for the purpose of correction. It is to effect behavioral change through advice, reproof, rebuke, and warning.

Paul frequently admonished his fellow Christians in his letters. He corrected the Corinthians because of division, immorality in the church, a smug attitude in the light of an immoral incident, saints going to law with each other, and disorders at the Lord's Table. He reproved those who questioned his apostleship (I Corinthians 4:14).

He warned the saints at Thessalonica who quit their jobs because they supposed the second coming of Christ was near that if a man didn't work he wouldn't eat (II Thessalonians 3:10). Paul openly rebuked Peter at Antioch for refusing to eat with Gentile Christians and thus undercutting the gospel of grace (Galatians 3:14ff).

Admonishment is the duty of not only leaders like Paul, but of every believer (I Thessalonians 5:12). Paul told the members of the church at Rome that they were "able to admonish one another" (Romans 15:14). He told the believers at Thessalonica to admonish an unruly brother (II Thessalonians 3:6).

Even church leaders may be reprimanded. Though an elder is not to be strongly rebuked (chastised with words) nor accused unless there are two or three witnesses (I Timothy 5:1,19), ministers should not mind being entreated "as a father."

One pastor tells how in his first church he decided so many pleas for offerings for drought-stricken areas in the western states had come across his desk that he would not mention the latest request. At the next church board meeting a deacon graciously asked the pastor if he had received a letter about a flood-stricken area in Kansas. The pastor replied in the affirmative but explained that he was sure the church had given all they could for such purposes, thus, he had done nothing with the letter.

Firmly but kindly the deacon replied, "Young man, you have no right to shield your congregation from a genuine need. If the people do not wish to give, that's their privilege, but you have no right to deny them the opportunity to give."

The pastor commented, "I was rebuked and have always been glad that I was."

Genuine building up of the church can be abetted by saints who are alert and sensitive to opportunities to admonish one another. The word for *admonish* is sometimes translated "counsel." If saints would counsel each other, some of the load would be taken off the shoulders of pastor, staff and professional counselors. The responsibility for ministering does not only point downward from pastor to people, but moves in a circle among believers, a "one another" affair.

A lady won a friend to Christ but became alarmed when the new convert invited a representative of a cult into her home to give a lesson. The friend phoned a kind warning which the new Christian took graciously; she then withdrew the invitation to the cultists.

A few weeks later the more mature Christian lady was

101

down in the dumps. Her recently converted friend phoned her, and with a mild rebuke quoted a verse to help overcome depression. Each had admonished the other in a helpful manner.

Taking the risk of admonishment is really a sign of friendship. When people care, they will correct. Too often today friendships develop tolerance to another's weakness, leaving little room for reprimand. One public leader said that half the crooked things men do in the secular world are done because people are afraid to be disagreeable to their so-called pals, who have deliberately developed pseudo-camaraderie designed to create an intimacy which can be taken advantage of. In genuine friendship we must resist the man who asks us to do a wrong thing. Christian brotherhood demands we speak the truth, but in love (Ephesians 4:15).

When people do not know each other well the tendency will be strong to suppress any difference of viewpoint; one will not want to suggest an improvement of conduct. Lack of interest in another leads to avoidance of confrontation—and thus, no admonishment. But, to refrain from interfering in the life of a fellow Christian may be thinly disguised indifference.

To the extent a brother cares for another brother, each will be solicitous for the other's growth and will risk confrontation to help build toward that end. The command to judge not forbids censorious condemnation and motive-impugning, but does not mean we should never make judgments. Some middle ground does exist between "playing God and playing dumb." Our responsibility is to develop the kind of mature relationship with others which will allow us to confront them caringly.

Charles Haddon Spurgeon tells of an unknown censor of great ability who used to send him a weekly list of his mispronunciations and other slips of speech. Spurgeon commented that he was greatly indebted to his critic for he was able to avoid repeating many mistakes.

How do you feel when someone reproves you? Does your ego rise to the defense? If we are letting God's searchlight probe our Christian life from day to day, we should not feel threatened when a fellow saint does the same. Supersensitivity to others' evaluation may indicate a closed mind to God's dealings with us. People really do appreciate frankness more than flattery, if offered in a loving manner.

John Calvin suffered a daring rebuke by William Farel, one of the earliest and boldest of the French Reformers. Calvin, who had been trained in law and the classics, did not by nature enjoy conflict and confrontation. After giving valuable assistance to the infant Reformation movement in Geneva, he determined to return to France to resume a sequestered life of study in the quiet of his library.

The night before his scheduled departure he met William Farel who told him in strong words, "You are just following your own wishes; and I declare in the name of Almighty God that if you refuse to take part in the Lord's work in this church God will curse the quiet life you want for your studies."

Calvin later acknowledged, "I felt as if God from heaven had laid His mighty hand upon me to stop me in my course . . . and I was so stricken with terror that I did not continue my journey."[15]

Thus, strong admonition by Farel kept Calvin in the thick of things at Geneva.

When we believe situations need correction we should personally confront the proper people. A mother complained to a deacon about the way junior church was run, exclaiming, "I don't want my son in that room. There's too much upset. I want him to learn something." The deacon asked if she had told the junior church superintendent how she felt.

"No," replied the mother, "I wouldn't want to hurt her feelings."

"But," replied the deacon, "you want me to tell her and I will hurt her feelings."

The deacon showed the mother that caring about the junior church program meant telling the superintendent. By refusing to be the bearer of a second-hand message, the deacon helped the mother face up to her responsibility. Even though it makes us uncomfortable, we should confront people with the truth in love.

Two qualifications for admonishing are given by Paul: possessing goodness and knowledge (Romans 15:14). One's own moral character, attitude, love, and desire to help are vital. Also required is a knowledge of the Scriptures and how to apply them in correcting misbehavior. "All scripture is given by inspiration of God, and is profitable for doctrine, for reproof, for correction, for instruction in righteousness: That the man of God may be perfect, throughly furnished unto all good works (II Timothy 3:16,17). To admonish is to bring God's word to bear on peoples' lives so as to expose sinful practices and to establish divinely-approved new patterns.

We must be sure our own lives are clean, however, before we attempt to admonish another. And we must do so in love—which is gentle—and in humility, restoring "in the spirit of meekness" anyone overtaken in a fault (Galatians 6:1).

ENCOURAGING

When David was a fugitive from King Saul, Jonathan, who loved David more deeply than a brother, found David's place of exile "and strengthened his hand in God. And he said unto him, Fear not: for the hand of Saul my father shall not find thee; and thou shalt be king over Israel . . ." (I Samuel 23:16,17). Brothers in the Lord are told to "exhort one another daily" (Hebrews 3:13). "Exhort" literally means "come alongside to help," and in noun form gives us one title of the Holy Spirit, the "Comforter" (John 14:16). We are to encourage each other often.

Some people seem to have the dubious gift of discouragement. Before Dr. Paul Tournier, Swiss Christian psychiatrist, published his first book he showed the manuscript to some friends. Because of their remarks, Tournier did nothing with the manuscript for six months. He was incapable of writing a single paragraph without at once considering it stupid. He had almost decided to give writing up altogether when he wondered how many books never saw the light of day because of the discouraging remarks of friends.

The person who disparages and discourages can easily turn a young life away from achievement and toward failure. But the right word can cheer the sad and lift the fallen. The Prophet Isaiah said, "The Lord God hath given me the tongue of the learned, that I should know how to speak a word in season to him that is weary" (Isaiah 50:4). "A wholesome tongue [word] is a tree of life" (Proverbs 15:4).

From the window of his second-floor studio in a downtown building, amidst the streaming traffic, an artist noticed that every morning a beggar took his place on the busy corner below. His clothes were tattered and dirty. His beard was overgrown, his hair disheveled. With plaintive gaze and pleading voice he begged for coins.

One morning the artist stood by the window and sketched the beggar, not as he looked but as he might have looked had he kept a good appearance and had a job. Then, opening the window, he beckoned the beggar to come up to the studio. When he entered, the artist showed him the canvas.

When the beggar asked, "Who is it?" the artist replied, "You. That is what I see in you." The astonished beggar thought a moment, then responded, "If that's the kind of man you see in me, that's the kind of man I'm going to be." Soon he had secured a position and was living respectably.

We need to look beyond the frailties and foibles of our fellow believers to see what they can become in Christ, then encourage them to realize their potential. The first time Christ met vacillating Simon, He called him by a new name, "Peter," which means rock—doubtless an encouragement to what Peter would become.

Even the strongest believer needs encouragement from time to time. Paul, who usually strengthened new believers, often needed support from fellow believers. For example, on his way to Rome to face Nero, apprehensive because of upcoming trial and possible execution if the verdict went against him, Paul was met several miles south of Rome by brethren who came from the capital. When Paul saw them he thanked God and took courage (Acts 28:14,15).

In an hour of sorrow especially we are to strengthen those who have lost a loved one. Speaking of the truth of the resurrection of the body and reunion at the coming of Christ, Paul said, "Wherefore comfort one another with these words" (I Thessalonians 4:18).

An older believer heard a young believer say, "I

remember what you said many years ago to me. It was a real help to my Christian life."

Replied the mature Christian, "Thank God for that, but I shudder to think how many times I have said wrong things to blossoming believers."

We are to encourage each other toward a better Christian life. Said the writer of Hebrews, "And let us consider one another to provoke unto love and to good works" (Hebrews 10:24). "Provoke" is used here not in the sense of "exasperate," but in the sense of "stimulate" or "fortify." We ought to call forth the best in others by helping them to see their gifts and hidden potential, and by urging them to take advantage of doing good.

Significantly, the command is linked to faithful church attendance. He adds, "Not forsaking the assembling of ourselves together" (verse 25). Though much encouragement may be given outside church services, formal meetings provide a source of mutual stimulation. Teaching, admonition and support may be given through the musical portion of the service, as well as through sharing of God's blessing, prayer for others' needs, and exposition of the Word.

A prisoner-of-war in Vietnam confessed that hours of prison solitude made him realize how much he needed the community of believers. He began to attend church regularly on his return to America.

The outstanding Baptist preacher, Dr. George W. Truett, was helping a struggling congregation raise money for their church building. They still needed $6,500. Truett found the response poor. With only $3,000 pledged, he said in exasperation, "Do you expect me to give the other $3,500 needed to reach your goal? I'm just a guest here today."

Suddenly, a woman near the back stood. Looking at

107

You Don't Have to Go It Alone

her husband seated on the platform recording pledges, she said in a shaking voice, "Charlie, I wonder if you would be willing for us to give our little home? We were offered exactly $3,500 cash for it yesterday. If the Saviour gave His life for us, wouldn't He be pleased if we made this sacrifice for Him?"

Truett reported that the fine husband responded with equal generosity. "Yes, Jennie, I was thinking the same thing." Turning to Truett, he said, "Brother Truett, if it's needed, we'll raise our pledge by $3,500."

Silence reigned for a few moments. Then some of the folks began to sob. Those who fifteen minutes earlier had refused to do more now either added their names to the list or increased their donations. In a short time their goal had been achieved, and Charlie and Jennie didn't have to forfeit their home. Their willingness to sacrifice had stimulated others to similar generosity.

It would be well for us to adopt the motto of a Long Island church, "Let us encourage one another."

EDIFICATION

The end result of teaching, admonishing, and encouraging is edification. Weather, sports, and business have their place in our lives, but continuous conversation on superficial matters prevents us from building up each other's lives. Paul urged church members to edify one another (Romans 14:19; I Thessalonians 5:11).

A young man, just a new Christian, idolized his second-hand souped-up jalopy. He spent hours working on the engine and shining the exterior. As he grew in his faith he realized that the car was an idol to him, and he asked two close pals who had led him to Christ to pray with him about this.

108

Three weeks later he shared with the youth leader, "Since I told those guys about my need to give less time to my hot rod, neither of them has checked up on me to ask how I'm doing. I cannot make it without them."

The youth leader said, "Tell them. They're responsible for you. You're all together in this."

After school on Monday, the young car owner cornered his two pals: "Do you care or not?"

The next Sunday he told his youth leader, "Were those guys ever smitten! Every day, and sometimes twice a day, they kept reminding me, 'Not too much time with that car, fellow.' "

Joan sensed a need for a regular quiet time for Bible study and prayer in her daily schedule. She shared her burden with several ladies in her Bible study. For the next several weeks, scarcely a day passed without one or two of those ladies phoning or stopping by to ask, "How's your quiet time coming, Joan?" They helped her build up a vital segment of her spiritual life.

Much edification comes through the spoken word, the ministry of conversation. Significantly, much of the tearing down against which Paul warns (Galatians 5:15) likewise results from the work of the tongue. We need to ask God to guard our tongues so that they may be used to build up, not break down.

9
Being Kind
One to Another

A Christian couple on a long trip stopped at a roadside rest area. For relaxation the husband practiced his trumpet for a few minutes. When they drove away, he forgot his instrument. Twenty minutes down the turnpike he exclaimed suddenly, "I left my trumpet back there!"

His wife retorted, "I know you did. I saw you leave it, but I didn't say anything because I wanted to teach you a lesson. Perhaps next time you'll not forget it."

As they drove back to retrieve the instrument, any potential lesson was likely nullified by resentment over his wife's lack of kindness.

Husbands and wives have been known to be mean to each other. A missionary, a guest for several days in a home, could not help but notice the almost continuous strain between husband and wife. Though they were truly

110

devoted to each other, the atmosphere was thick with harsh attitude and unkind words.

In a public survey asking the question, "What is your leading complaint against your mate?" the most frequent answer was bad disposition—being unpleasant, moody, irritable, rotten-tempered or just plain ornery.

Strangely, some who know their Bibles well sometimes act cantankerously. A man gifted in Bible exposition was unbelievably rude, lacking the kindly graces of the Spirit in his dealings with fellow workers. One would derive most benefit from his public ministry if he did not see his private manners.

We are not to be nasty, but nice to one another. Paul put it this way, "Let all bitterness, and wrath, and anger, and clamour, and evil speaking, be put away from you, with all malice: And be ye kind one to another, tender-hearted, forgiving one another, even as God for Christ's sake hath forgiven you" (Ephesians 4:31,32).

NASTINESS TO BE PUT OFF

Those first five nouns of verse 31—bitterness, wrath, anger, clamor, evil speaking—progress from an inner spirit of bitterness and anger to an outward manifestation of loud, insulting speech.

Peter spoke of the "gall of bitterness" (Acts 8:23). No bilious disposition should be displayed by believers. The writer of Hebrews warns against letting the root of bitterness spring up to trouble and defile others (Hebrews 12:15), thus spoiling the peace which we are to pursue (verse 14).

Not only does bitterness disrupt relationships with others but it poisons its possessor, like a cornered rattlesnake which sometimes becomes so angry it bites itself.

111

You Don't Have to Go It Alone

Spitefulness and hate do deeper harm to the carrier than to the recipient, freezing reason and response, eating acidly from within, making us critical, cynical, and caustic.

Seventeenth-century baroque sculptors of Italy often allowed their bitter attitudes to be expressed in their works. In Rome today stands Bernini's lovely Fountain of Rivers. He despised Borromini, designer of the Church of St. Agnes, situated opposite the fountain. To deliberately insult Borromini, sculptor Bernini carved one of the statues in the fountain group with a hand covering its eyes as though it could not stand to look at the church. Then, to add insult to injury, he fashioned another figure with its hands up in panic as if it were afraid the church might fall on it.

That was 300 years ago in Italy. Here's an incident from our own land in this century. A church which was putting up an addition close to a lady's property needed her permission to trespass on her land so the workmen could build more easily. When she refused permission, the workmen had to work from inside their new structure, which made the labor harder and longer.

In retaliation, the church erected a fence on its own property which somehow kept the lady from using her garage. For years bitterness kept the church board from voting to take down the fence, thus rendering the neighbor's garage virtually useless.

Husbands, in particular, are told not to be bitter against their wives (Colossians 3:19). Too often, we are meanest to those to whom we are the closest. Mates should not be resentful of nor exasperated with each other, dyspeptically nursing grievances. Such feelings can flare forth in fury on the loved one and on innocent parties nearby.

The Los Angeles police department reported that during one considerable period, 80 percent of the morning rush-hour accidents were caused by people who had earlier been involved in arguments with their mates before leaving home.

Wrath (temporary, emotional outbursts) and anger (settled, intentional state) are two words which are often joined in non-biblical Greek. These emotions can issue in loud, boisterous railing and insulting talk. Perhaps in a church business meeting someone with an opposite view, through political maneuvering outwits and outvotes your viewpoint, stirring in you the urge to become bitter, and to let go with some vituperative name-calling. Paul says we are not to yield to such inclination, but to put such malice from us.

Two pike were found in the Sault Ste. Marie canal in southern Canada with their jaws locked together after a fight to the death. Came the comment, "That sadly is how many a friendship ends—in a deadlock! What some people believe is not mouth-to-mouth 'resuscitation' but mouth-to-mouth 'mortification.' When you find two people locked in mortal combat, check their mouths. They have probably been in a verbal conflict somewhere along the line."[14]

A minister was called to a church where a very inconsequential matter had split the congregation into two parts. As the new pastor began to visit his new membership, each side tried to persuade him to their viewpoint. But he immediately replied, "Excuse me, but I did not come to hear that. Mr. Jones is a friend of mine, and you wouldn't want me to hear anything derogatory about him. Let's read from the Bible." Then he would pray.

When he left the home, the people felt rebuked, but with kindness. He did the same in all the homes so that

113

nobody could get his ear, and all felt ashamed. Soon the fire died down. People began to be kind to each other, again bringing the blessing of God on the church.

NICENESS TO BE PUT ON

Christianity is not based on negatives, but on positives. Paul never stops with just renunciation; we are not merely to be rid of hate, but to be filled with love. We are to put off nastiness and put on niceness. We are to be kind to one another, tenderhearted, forgiving one another.

Let us consider kindness. The word *kind* in Ephesians 4:32 is translated "good" in I Corinthians 15:33, "gracious" in I Peter 2:3, and "easy," as opposed to "burdensome" and "pressing" in Matthew 11:30. In its noun form it is often translated "kindness" (II Corinthians 6:6; Ephesians 2:7; Colossians 3:12; Titus 3:4), "goodness" (Romans 2:4), and only once (and this is in the list of the Spirit's fruit) "gentleness" (Galatians 5:22).

Kindness is manifested in goodness, a pleasant benevolence. This virtue may be aptly translated "gentle kindness." Some doctors and nurses tend to press more tenderly than do others on sore areas. Such medical personnel possess a gentle kindness.

Kind is thought to be etymologically derived from "kin-ned," denoting the affection of kindred or brother. Kindness involves courtesy, thoughtfulness, mildness, as opposed to harshness, sharpness, and bitterness. Some people exhibit a goodness that is precise, prim, and proper, but which needs to be tempered by sweetness, for it is possible to be kind in an unkind way, such as running an errand begrudgingly. We can understand the little girl who prayed, "Lord, make all the bad people good, and all the good people nice."

114

To be kind is to be good-natured, disposed toward being helpful and considerate, such as not forgetting to write down a phone message for another in your house; and desirous of giving pleasure or relief, such as the Good Samaritan and Dorcas, who sewed garments for the poor widows of Joppa. In the Old Testament the Kenites showed kindness to the Israelites in their flight from Egypt (I Samuel 15:6; Judges 1:16). Joseph asked his fellow prisoner, the butler, "to shew kindness" by mentioning him before Pharaoh (Genesis 40:14).

Kindness in speech will rule out barbs, innuendo, sarcasm, and biting, curt replies, and will rule in the soft answer. We have no record of Jesus ever commenting in a derogatory manner on anyone's physical appearance, such as calling Zacchaeus "shorty" or "shrimp."

A smart question to ask ourselves before letting statements pass our lips is, "Is it kind?" This might prevent many a remark that withers a groping self-image and emotionally cuts down an aspiring person to below size, such as, "You'll never make the honor roll," or "You'll never be able to make a cake," or "You'll just never be satisfied."

Former nun Susan Hermes cites the influence of her business supervisor as a major contributing factor in her coming to Christ. Released from the convent because of a nervous breakdown, and requiring psychiatric treatment for several years, in financial desperation she took a job as a bookkeeper. Her supervisor was different from any other person she had ever known—even-tempered, patient and understanding.

In the early weeks of her employment, Susan asked if she could work through her lunch hour to get off early for a psychiatrist's appointment in late afternoon. Her supervisor told her she could take both her usual lunch hour and get off early. Moreover, she could take off early any time for such appointments without the need of working through lunch.

Such kindness soon led Susan to open her heart to her supervisor, sharing her deep fear of serious relapse because she could no longer afford psychiatric treatments. The supervisor suggested Susan see her pastor who later led her to Christ.

Interestingly, this word kindness is used in connection with all three members of the Trinity: of the Father (Romans 2:4); of the Son (Colossians 3:12,13); and of the Spirit (II Corinthians 6:6). No wonder from such inner kindness flow the countless loving, merciful, and gracious acts of the Triune God!

Gentle kindness will enable us to have "Peace one with another" (Mark 9:50). At a private school in England, if two boys are caught fighting they are tied together for one day, to eat, work, walk, and play together. The procedure, which has cured many a conflict, is based on the conviction that disagreement stems from the fact that we do not really know each other. Acts of kindness toward another can develop a closer relationship, thus helping us to "be of the same mind one toward another" (Romans 12:16).

Gentle kindness will help us to "wash one another's feet" (John 13:14). A visiting professor gave three addresses at a large American university where he was accorded great respect. After the series he returned to his home city to "bus" tables at a coffeehouse sponsored by his home church. The night was busy and hectic. As he was hurrying to clear a table, a customer snapped his fingers, calling in an arrogant tone, "Hey, boy!" His first reaction was the thought, "Doesn't he know who I am? I don't have to serve in here." But he quickly overcame his initial reaction and proceeded to act in kindness.

Gentle kindness will help us serve one another in love (Galatians 5:13).

Wheaton College president Dr. Hudson T. Armerding tells of the summer in 1947 when he and his wife were in the candidate school conducted by what was then known as the China Inland Mission. They had one child with a second on the way. After a weekend of visiting relatives in New Jersey, they returned to the mission headquarters in Philadelphia with an extensive load of luggage. As they prepared to unload their automobile, the secretary of the mission ran down from his office to carry the bulk of the suitcases up to their room. The mission executive could have called on one of the staff or a houseboy; instead, he did it himself.

Gentle kindness will rebuke when necessary, but always with a mild manner. Charles H. Spurgeon, Baptist minister of London, England, had a preacher-friend, Dr. Newman Hall, who wrote a book entitled, *Come to Jesus*. Another preacher published an article in which he ridiculed Hall, who bore it patiently for a while. But when the article gained popularity, Hall sat down and wrote a letter of protest. His answer was full of retaliatory invectives that outdid anything in the article which attacked him. Before mailing the letter, Hall took it to Spurgeon for his opinion.

Spurgeon read it carefully then, handing it back, asserted it was excellent and that the writer of the article deserved it all. "But," he added, "it just lacks one thing." After a pause Spurgeon continued, "Underneath your signature you ought to write the words, 'Author of *Come to Jesus.*' "

The two godly men looked at each other for a few minutes. Then Hall tore the letter to shreds.

117

You Don't Have to Go It Alone

Then there is tenderheartedness. We have noted that the kindness commanded in Ephesians 4:32 is a gentle kindness. The quality of that gentleness is now reinforced by the word, tenderhearted. In New Testament times, emotions were linked to various parts of the body. *Tenderhearted* here literally means "having strong bowels." It could be translated, "strongly compassionate."

Just below the veneer of civilization lies the savagery of the human heart which erupts into acts of man's inhumanity to man. Witness the concentration camps of World War II, and the cruel tortures by nations even today. In general, humanity is rough and tough, hard-boiled and calloused, often indifferent toward those in distress despite flights of philanthropic magnificence in times of major disasters.

How easy it is for an unsympathetic spirit to creep into our lives. We become emotionally jaded by the staggering weight of the world's woes which are dumped into our living room daily via press and TV. When we learn of a brother's need it is convenient to shrug it off with a careless, "Too bad, but everybody has his trouble!"

Selfishly wrapped up in our own interests we fail to extend a helping hand to the needy. What we need is a hide like an elephant, and a heart like a dove—a thick skin to ward off the barbs and slights of others, and a spirit that is soft and sensitive to the troubles of others.

Peter commanded that we be full of pity. The King James Version renders the word "tenderhearted" in Ephesians 4:32 as "pitiful" in I Peter 3:8. The verb form is frequently rendered, "moved with compassion."

Compassion was certainly a recurring emotion of the Lord Jesus Christ. The Prophet Isaiah said Christ would grow up "as a tender plant" (Isaiah 53:2), that He would

118

"gather the lambs with his arm, and . . . gently lead those . . . with young" (Isaiah 40:11), and that "A bruised reed shall he not break" (Isaiah 42:3). A bruised reed we would likely trample underfoot, but Jesus would give it special, tender care.

How often Jesus was moved with compassion for both multitudes and individuals because they fainted and were scattered shepherdless (Matthew 9:36), because they were sick (Matthew 14:14), because they were hungry (Matthew 15:32), because they were blind (Matthew 20:34), because they were leprous (Mark 1:40,41). Compassion on a widow prompted Him to raise her only son from the dead (Luke 7:12-14). Compassion caused Him to shed tears at the grave of Lazarus (John 11:35), and over the city of Jerusalem (Luke 19:41).

Now at the right hand of the Father, this High Priest bids us come boldly to the throne of grace because He has been touched with the feeling of our infirmities (Hebrews 4:15,16). James sums it up thus: "The Lord is very pitiful, and of tender mercy" (James 5:11). We are to be like Him.

A young man went to collect the rent on a property his parents had left him. He found a widow and her sick girl barely eking out an existence. Not only did he notify their church and Social Services who came to the rescue, but out of compassion he did not take any rent from these unfortunate folks the many years they remained in his property.

Some years ago a retired nurse visited the baby ward of a large hospital where once she had been a mainstay. Looking at a baby's chart, she was puzzled by an entry she had never seen, "TLC, three times daily." The baby was bluish, shriveled and two months old. The same entry appeared on the chart of a vigorous, pinkish baby. She wondered if TLC was a new wonder drug, but was too proud to ask the young supervisor.

When a nurse picked up a baby and fondled it for several minutes, the older nurse worried over the possibility of infection. Alone momentarily, she peered through the prescription cabinet but found no TLC. Finally, she cornered an intern. "Doctor, what's this new medicine, TLC?"

The doctor grinned, led her into the baby ward again, then pointed to a happy, cooing infant. He explained, "A month ago this baby was a sack of bones, not expected to live. Medicines did no good. It was TLC that caused the change; it's not from a bottle but it's the greatest medicine for babies ever discovered. Some die without it. It stands for Tender Loving Care."

If TLC is necessary for a child's normal growth, or even survival, how much more vital is tender kindness in our dealings with God's children? A weather-beaten tombstone in an old cemetery read merely, "He was compassionate." This long-gone stranger had the kind of heart God wants us to have.

Another Christian positive is forgiveness. Instead of reacting to injury with bitterness and vituperation, we are to respond with forgiveness. The perfect model of forgiveness is God, who has every right to be angry and vengeful against us for all our sins against Him, yet He extends forgiveness through the atoning work of Christ. As Paul puts it, we should be "forgiving one another, even as God for Christ's sake hath forgiven you" (Ephesians 4:32).

Interestingly, kindness is mentioned several times in the Bible against a backdrop of unkindness. Jesus, in commanding love to enemies, added that God is "kind unto the unthankful and to the evil" (Luke 6:35).

Jonathan asked David to show kindness to him and his house despite the fact that the head of that house and Jonathan's father, King Saul, would treat David shabbily (I Samuel 20:14,15). Years later when David's kingdom was established, David asked, "Is there not yet any [that is left] of the house of Saul, that I may shew the kindness of God unto him?" As a result, Jonathan's son, lame Mephibosheth was brought to Jerusalem where he ate regularly at the king's table (II Samuel 9:3,7).

In the famous love chapter Paul wrote that love "suffereth long, and is kind" (I Corinthians 13:4). Under provocation, hate prompts desire for revenge, but under love kindness will desire to do the enemy good.

A U.S. pilot shot down in Vietnam and taken prisoner told how, as his captors dragged him through many villages with his hands tied tightly behind his back, the villagers shouted obscenities and hurled objects at him. In the midst of the abuse he felt someone press something into his hand. Closing his fingers over the object, he held on. Hours later, when his hands were finally untied he found a crumbled cookie in his palm. Then he remembered that the village girl who had pressed the bit of food into his hand had caught his eye as she retreated into the crowd. When she saw him looking at her, she made the sign of the cross.

In the face of unkindness we are to be kind. A slave who had been given his freedom settled in New England and became a respected citizen. However, in church he had to sit in the segregated gallery and was never allowed to partake of the Lord's Supper. When he died he left part of his savings to the church to buy a silver communion plate.

Bishop Festo Kivengere, who fled Uganda after his church's archbishop was apparently murdered along with

121

You Don't Have to Go It Alone

hundreds of other Christians was asked how believers should pray. He answered that we should pray that the Christians in Uganda would be kept from bitterness and that they would cover the bleeding wounds of Uganda with the love of Christ.

In a Peanuts' cartoon Lucy addressed Snoopy, "There are times when you really bug me, but I must admit there are also times when I feel like giving you a hug."

Snoopy replied, "That's the way I am, hugable and bugable."

The apostle is saying, "Don't be bugable, but hugable. Not nasty, but nice."

10

Being Non-Judgmental
One of Another

Before his audience, a lecturer held up a large surface of pure white, marred by one tiny blot. "What do you see?" he asked.

"A blot," was the almost unanimous answer. Few saw the white background. How like human nature! We are quick to see the defects in others.

Cautioning against the practice of looking for the blot in a fellow believer, Paul wrote, "Let us not therefore judge one another any more" (Romans 14:13). Christ pointedly warned against a critical attitude in the Sermon on the Mount. "Judge not, that ye be not judged" (Matthew 7:1).

THE NATURE OF THE JUDGING FORBIDDEN

These commands do not mean that civil courts are to

123

be abolished or that evil must be tolerated. Nor do they mean that Christians should never confront and admonish fellow believers, for there are occasions when blots must be judged. For example, Christian in *Pilgrim's Progress* was perfectly justified in criticizing Talkative for his hypocrisy. But the command does prohibit the censoring spirit which impugns the motives of others on insufficient grounds or reaches hasty conclusions. The mental exercise of jumping to conclusions can be a dangerous practice, according to this anonymous doggerel:

> There was a dog named August,
> He was always jumping at conclusions;
> One day he jumped at the conclusion of a mule,
> That was the last day of August.

False conclusions are easily drawn from hasty premises. Motives are often questioned. "The reason he gave such a nice check to the church is because he wants to reduce his income tax," suggests a neighbor. The eager reporting of another's detraction may be a form of subtle, indirect criticism.

Aaron and Miriam criticized their brother Moses. "Hath the Lord indeed spoken only by Moses?" (Numbers 12:2). The Lord's anger was kindled against Aaron and Miriam and Miriam was stricken with leprosy for seven days. Miriam was guilty of evil-speaking against her brother, whom she had watched over when he was a baby in the ark in the bulrushes. Tragically, loved ones are a frequent target of our unkind remarks.

When the King of Ammon died, King David sent messengers to convey expressions of sympathy to the late monarch's son, Hanun. But Hanun falsely concluded that the messengers had come to spy out and overthrow his kingdom, not to console, with the result that he shaved David's messengers and partially disrobed them. Learning of the humiliating mistreatment of his messengers, David was incensed and slew 7,000 Ammonites in battle (I Chronicles 19).

Paul was once accused of desecrating the temple in Jerusalem by those who had jumped to conclusions. Paul had been spotted on the streets of the city in company with some Gentiles. Later, when they saw him in the temple with a stranger, they immediately inferred that the stranger was one of the same Gentiles with whom they had previously seen him. Paul was beaten almost to the point of death (Acts 21:27ff).

Secular life abounds with examples of people jumping to conclusions, some of them humorous. A lady invited several friends to a mushroom steak dinner. When her maid opened a can of mushrooms, she discovered a slight scum on the top. Since the guests were expected momentarily, the lady of the house suggested, "Give the dog a little and if he eats it, it's probably all right." The dog licked it eagerly and begged for more, so the dinner was quickly completed.

After the main course, the maid came in to serve the dessert, but her face was ashen white. She whispered into her employer's ear, "Ma'am, the dog's dead."

There was only one thing to do and the lady did it. Some time later, after the doctor had left, the guests were reclining in various stages of recovery from the use of the stomach pump. The lady called the maid and asked, "Where's the poor dog now?" Came the answer, "Out on the front steps, Ma'am, where he fell after the car hit him."

Hasty judging can bring sad consequences. An older couple brought a little boy home from a children's shelter

125

for a weekend, with the thought of possible adoption. The day went beautifully. But candies which the couple kept in a paper bag at the head of their bed were missing the next morning. The lad maintained he had not left his room across the hall. Neither threat nor promise could elicit a confession of guilt. So silently and sadly the couple drove the boy back to the children's shelter and left him.

That night they could not sleep. Suddenly, out of the stillness the rustling of the paper bag containing the candy told its own story. The thief was a mouse. Long before daylight they arose and sped away to bring the happy child home for good.

A few years ago gifts to the Prairie Bible Institute of Alberta, Canada, declined from a certain geographical area. At that time the school's president, Dr. Maxwell, had undergone two operations for cataracts, one on each eye. When a representative of the school was visiting in that particular area, he was approached by a donor as to why Dr. Maxwell was riding around in two Cadillacs. Hasty jumping to conclusions had changed cataracts to Cadillacs and caused people to withhold their gifts.[16]

THE DANGERS OF JUDGING

Passing judgments on flimsy foundation may have damaging implications Godward, selfward, and manward. By judging we assume the place and prerogatives of God.

The main character in a play entitled, "The Man Who Played God," was a deaf man who lived in an apartment high above Central Park in New York City. Using powerful binoculars, he read the lips of people sitting on benches several stories below. To those with trouble he sent a butler with word that help was on the way. If the park bench occupants asked the source of this help, the butler would reply, "It comes from the man who plays God." In this play, benevolence was exercised to everyone by the man playing God, but in real life playing God causes harm to others and ourselves.

Only God can judge. When we pass judgment on the motives of others, we are presuming a divine prerogative, for no human being can read the mind and purposes of fellow human beings. We are virtually saying, "God, I'm climbing up on Your throne beside You. Shove over, for I, too, see why people act as they do. I'm as capable to judge as you are."

God's Word speaks often against judging. Paul wrote, "But why dost thou judge thy brother? or why dost thou set at nought thy brother? for we shall all stand before the judgment seat of Christ. For it is written, As I live, saith the Lord, every knee shall bow to me, and every tongue shall confess to God . . . Let us not therefore judge one another any more" (Romans 14:10,11,13).

James warned, "Speak not evil one of another, brethren. He that speaketh evil of his brother, and judgeth his brother, speaketh evil of the law, and judgeth the law: but if thou judge the law, thou art not a doer of the law, but a judge" (James 4:11).

Speaking evil against a brother implies that the law is inadequate in its judgment. Also, condemning a brother is the function of a judge. The ultimate Judge is the Giver of the Law, who is none other than God Himself, "who is able to save and to destroy: who art thou that judgest another?" (verse 12). Who dares to usurp the office of the Supreme Judge by speaking evil of a brother?

By judging we declare ourselves a candidate for judgment. A young man with an exaggerated opinion of his

You Don't Have to Go It Alone

own abilities was standing in front of a taxidermist's store. An owl in the window attracted many sightseers. Anxious to show off his knowledge, the young man said with a pompous air, "Well, if I couldn't stuff an owl better than that, I'd quit the business. The head isn't right. The pose of the body isn't right. The feet are not placed right." Just as he finished his judgment, the owl turned his head and winked at him. The crowd laughed.

The critic becomes unpopular for he invites criticism, thus making himself the target of derisive or revengeful human nature. Jesus said, "Judge not, that ye be not judged. For with what judgment ye judge, ye shall be judged: and with what measure ye mete, it shall be measured to you again" (Matthew 7:1,2).

Often, the one who criticizes broadcasts his need of judgment, for criticism usually indicates feelings of inferiority and becomes an instrument for raising self-esteem. When we feel beneath a person, fallen human nature sometimes wants to drag him down. Thus, judging shows we are on a lower level and in need of improvement. Criticism gives, at the cheapest rate, the feeling of equality or superiority.

In dwelling on the flaws of others there looms the danger of self-complacency. The critic blindly concludes with the Pharisee, "I thank thee, that I am not as other men" (Luke 18:11).

Judging others foreshadows a more dreadful judgment to come. Korah and the 250 princes who spoke against Moses were swallowed up by the earth (Numbers 16).

Some early saints who suffered for their witness observed other saints of their acquaintance escaping persecution. The tendency was to pass judgment. "They're trimming their testimony. They aren't as zealous as I am or else they would be hauled before the

128

courts just as I've been arrested!" But James wrote, "Grudge not one against another, brethren, lest ye be condemned: Behold, the judge standeth before the door" (James 5:9). The day would come when the Judge of the universe would punish those who had persecuted them, would correctly decide as to whether or not their fellow believers had trimmed their testimony, and also would take note of any irritability or spirit of censure on their part.

By judging we injure others and our collective Christian testimony. Someone said, "The hammer is the only knocker that does any good." A young fellow who had been invited by a Christian friend to attend a gospel service accepted Christ as his Savior. On the way home from the meeting, the young fellows ran into a couple of fine Christian ladies who had been present at the service.

"How did you like the message?" asked the young men whereupon the ladies passed a harsh criticism of the preacher. The young man who had made a profession of faith that night was evidently startled, and for many years rarely darkened the door of a church.

At Sunday dinner, roast beef makes a good dish, as do roast pork or roast lamb. But roast preacher is undesirable. If we would have our children and friends respect the preacher, we had better not find fault with him in their hearing. Many children have been turned away from the gospel by the free and easy criticism of the preacher over the dinner table at home. Neither should we serve roast Sunday school teacher, roast soloist, or roast organist. We can't build up the Lord's work while tearing down respect for His workers.

You Don't Have to Go It Alone

Constructive criticism has its rightful place, but much criticism is destructive. A man criticized another for his methods of giving out tracts. "How do *you* do it?" asked the tract distributer. "Er . . . ah . . . I don't," came the embarrassed reply of the critic. The evangelism worker retorted, "I like the way I do it better than the way you don't."

The spirit of censure should be defeated. The following suggestions will help to overcome it.

Remember that all of us have faults which are liable to honest criticism. A tenant complained to his landlord about the noisy neighbor upstairs who often stamped on the floor and shouted till after midnight. Then he added, "But it doesn't bother me too much for I usually stay up and practice the tuba until about that time every night anyway!"

All of us have flaws which could provide legitimate grounds for criticism by others. To the accusers of the woman taken in adultery Jesus said, "He that is without sin among you, let him first cast a stone at her" (John 8:7). But it is far easier to see faults in others than in ourselves. We more quickly see a smudge on someone else's face than on our own. Little faults in others loom large in our vision, while large faults in ourselves appear small. Like the Quaker who said to his wife, "Everybody in this world is a bit queer except thee and me, and sometimes I think thee a bit queer."

Or as the couplet goes:

> Faults in others I can see;
> But praise the Lord there's none in me.

The poet Burns had some wise words:

> O wad some Power the giftie gie us,
> To see oursels as ithers see us.

If we did see ourselves as others see us, we might be more inclined to say with a character in Shakespeare's "As You Like It": "I will chide no brother in the world but myself, against whom I know most faults."

Strange as it may seem, we often judge others for the identical faults we possess. Jesus spoke of a man with a beam in his eye judging another who had a mote in his eye. Reduced to language which emphasizes the irony of the scene, Jesus was saying, "Here's a fellow with a tree trunk protruding from his eye who is criticizing another who has a little sliver in his eye. First cast the tree trunk out of your eye. Then you'll see clearly to get the sliver out of the other fellow's eye."

The ten disciples who so vehemently criticized the two disciples whose mother had asked for the places of honor for her sons in the coming kingdom probably had the same thing in mind for themselves.

In "Romeo and Juliet," after a feud between the Capulets and the Montagues, the two families were forbidden to cause any more street brawls on pain of death. Mercuratio, friend of the Montagues, accused one of the Capulets of being quarrelsome, but within ten minutes after making such an accusation, Mercuratio himself was guilty of fostering a quarrel with the nephew of the Capulets who chanced along the street, and was himself killed in the brawl.

A little boy yelled angrily at his big brother, "You're mean and selfish! You took the last apple and I wanted it!"

You Don't Have to Go It Alone

A lady was showing a friend her neighbor's wash through her back window. "Our neighbor isn't very clean. Look at those streaks on the wash!" Said her friend, "Those streaks aren't on your neighbor's wash. They're on your window."

Your neighbor's wash looks a great deal better when your windows are clean! So before flaring up at anyone else's faults, count to ten—ten of your own.

Reflect that you might be guilty of the same fault given the same circumstances. Given similar circumstances, perhaps someday you too might fall into the same pitfall. Hence the advice: "Brethren, if a man be overtaken in a fault, ye which are spiritual, restore such an one in the spirit of meekness; considering thyself, lest thou also be tempted" (Galatians 6:1).

When you see the errors of others and cannot understand why they could do such things, remember that perhaps they cannot comprehend why you do the things you do. If you were in their shoes and a product of the same background, you too might easily be guilty of their faults.

Years ago, it was the custom of some Indian tribes to appoint judges who traveled a circuit of villages to try cases. Every judge was required to walk in the forest alone and pray this prayer, "O Great Spirit, Maker of men, forbid that I judge any man until I have walked for two moons in his moccasins."

Pray don't find fault with the man who limps,
Or stumbles along the road,
Unless you have worn the shoes he wears
Or struggled beneath his load.

There may be tacks in his shoes that hurt,

132

Though hidden away from view,
Or the burdens he bears, placed on your back,
Might cause you to stumble too.
—*Author Unknown*

We should try to think of another's good points rather than the bad. It is a good idea to play the game of Christian cancellation. When someone speaks of the blot, point out the white background.

Two boys were speaking of another lad. "He's so slow in baseball," said the first boy.

"Yes," replied the other, "but he always plays fair."

"But he's so stupid at school," retorted the first.

"Yes," came the defense, "but he always studies hard."

Every unkind word spoken by the first boy was cancelled by the second one.

Ben Franklin had a friend with a deformed leg who used to determine whether or not a stranger would make a good companion by his attitude toward the lame leg. If the stranger gave undue emphasis to his bad leg, he would have nothing further to do with him. If minor mention was given the bad leg, the stranger would be considered suitable for friendship.

A girl who had been working two months for a Christian company wasn't surprised when one of the top bosses wanted to see her. Confused by the clamoring phones, the sudden demands for information and by working on different matters simultaneously, she knew she was less than efficient.

In his office the boss leafed through all the papers which she was sure listed all her failings. But he looked up, smiling. "Your supervisor tells me you get along very well with people. I wonder if this isn't the area of your

133

skills. You could be of service to us in the personnel department. Would you be willing to try it there?"

The girl left his office inwardly singing. The supervisor had kindly ignored her obvious deficiencies. Instead he had concentrated on her strong points. The company now had a contented employee, quite suited to her new job.

John Wesley and a preacher friend of plain manners were once invited to dinner where the host's daughter, noted for her beauty, had been profoundly impressed by Wesley's preaching. During a pause in the meal Wesley's friend took hold of the young lady's hand and, lifting it, called attention to the sparkling rings she wore. "What do you think of this, sir, for a Methodist hand?"

The girl turned crimson. Wesley likewise was embarrassed for his aversion to jewelry was well-known. With a quiet, benevolent smile, he simply said, "The hand is beautiful."

The young lady appeared at the evening service without her jewels and became a strong Christian.

Remember that we don't know all the facts and are therefore incompetent to pass correct judgment. One reason we find fault is because we don't have all the facts. A man in a Pullman car couldn't get to sleep because of a crying baby in the care of a young father. So he thundered out, "Why don't you take that baby to its mother so the rest of us can get some sleep?"

The young father replied, "I wish I could. But the baby's mother, my wife, died yesterday. Her body is in the baggage car ahead. We're taking her back to her old home for burial."

Immediately the man was all apologies, climbed out of his berth, and took care of the baby so that the broken-hearted father could get some sleep.

The task of a judge is never easy, even when much of

the evidence is available. Human judgment is fallible. We know so little of the private life of our church's fellow members, even though they may share some burdens. Perhaps that deacon's business isn't good. Or that Sunday school teacher's health is poor. Or that choir member's husband isn't congenial. Or the usher's daughter away at college is in trouble. If we knew the extenuating circumstances, we would be more understanding of certain conduct. If we had a full explanation, we might be sorry we judged. We don't have to give account of our fellow church member's behavior at the throne of God. Everyone shall give account of himself, not his brother.

A lady boarded a streetcar and asked the conductor to let her off at a certain corner. He promised to do so, but he forgot until the car had passed her street by two blocks. Then he quickly told her. As she descended from the streetcar, she gave him a violent tongue-lashing. He answered not a word.

A passenger standing nearby asked the conductor how he could take such a flow of abuse without retaliation. He replied, "It's true I was to blame for forgetting the street, but that lady doesn't know that I have a sick wife at home—so sick she needs both day and night nurses. I have a day nurse there while I work but I can't afford a night nurse. So I've been staying up with her all night. I've done that the last two nights. And I've worked every day because I need the money to pay the day nurse. So I haven't had a wink of sleep the last 48 hours. That's why my memory isn't working so well. But that lady doesn't know that."

A member of a church missionary committee rose to his feet several times during a two-hour meeting, stood behind his chair, and looked at the pictures on the wall behind him. At the end of the session another member of the committee took it upon himself to lecture the peripatetic for his lack of attention.

The man replied, "Recently I've developed a back problem. Doctors tell me I must change my position every half hour, otherwise my back stiffens up and becomes very sore. When I do get up and look at pictures, I'm listening very carefully."

When a Christian heard a fellow believer was criticizing him, the Christian went directly to him. "Will you be kind enough to tell me my faults to my face so that I may profit from your honesty and try to overcome them?"

The other agreed. Then the first brother said, "First let's pray together, asking the Lord to open my eyes to my faults. You please lead."

After the prayer the second believer said, "After praying over the matter, it looks like your faults are so minor they're not worth talking about. The truth is I feel now that in going around talking against you I have been serving the devil. Really, I have need for you to pray for me and forgive me the wrong I've done you."

The habit of constantly criticizing violates Scripture and dissipates spiritual vitality. John Wesley said, "Methodists are to be governed by the following rule: Do not mention the fault of an absent person, in particular, of ministers or of those in authority."

A person who claims to be spiritual and bridleth not his tongue is deceived as to his own spirituality. But "A word fitly spoken is like apples of gold in pictures of silver" (Proverbs 25:11).

11
Greeting One Another

The way people greet one another differs widely around the world. In parts of Saudi Arabia as soon as a guest arrives it is the custom to produce a brazier with incense burning on the charcoal in order to perfume the room.

In northern Nigeria friends used to salute each other by placing thumb and forefinger against those of the other person, then cracking them. Older men greeted one another by pulling each other's beards.

In one clan in South Africa, salutations were generally accompanied by a clapping of hands. Men beat their hands against each other, placing them parallel. Women did the same, but they placed them crosswise or at right angles. In another tribe a man would give a greeting by bowing down and clasping his hands at the height of his knees, either on the right side or the left.

In still another part of the world a host will wave to his

guest with the flat of his hand. The guest must make a similar response. Another custom calls for a person to place his right hand between the extended palms of the person saluted.

In a part of East Africa a few decades ago courtesy demanded that a man spit into the palm of his hand before offering it to a friend.

CUSTOMARY GREETING IN BIBLE TIMES

In Bible times and lands, the common greeting among family and friends was a kiss, as it is also today in some parts of Europe, Asia and the Middle East. Isaac, while mistakenly giving the blessing to Jacob, asked for a kiss (Genesis 27:26,27). Jacob kissed Cousin Rachel on meeting her for the first time (Genesis 29:11). Learning his sister's son had come, Laban ran and kissed him (Genesis 29:13). When Esau was reunited with his brother Jacob, he "fell on his neck and kissed him" (Genesis 33:4). Joseph kissed all his brothers when he dramatically revealed himself to them in Egypt (Genesis 45:15). When Moses returned from his forty years in the desert of Midian, Aaron met him partway and kissed him (Exodus 4:27). At their farewell Jonathan and David kissed and wept (I Samuel 20:41).

How deeply the woman of the street had already come to love her Savior when, washing His feet with her tears and wiping them with her hair, she repeatedly kissed those feet (Luke 7:38,45). In the parable, the father kissed the prodigal son on his repentant return (Luke 15:20). Judas' kiss of betrayal was all the more treacherous, coming from one who was so close to Jesus (Matthew 26:48,49).

It is not surprising then to see that in that culture

members of the early local church warmly recognized each other as members of the same family of God and expressed their greeting with a kiss. After Paul's tender farewell speech to the Ephesian elders, they all wept profusely and kissed him (Acts 20:37). Since this was the common custom, it was not strange then that five times in the New Testament the letters end with instructions to salute or greet one another with a kiss, four times called "an holy kiss" by Paul (Romans 16:16; I Corinthians 16:20; II Corinthians 13:12; I Thessalonians 5:26), and once "a kiss of charity" by Peter (I Peter 5:14).

About the middle of the second century, Justin Martyr wrote concerning new converts, "After we have thus baptized the one who has been convinced and has given his assent to our teaching, we bring him to the place where those who are called *brothers* are gathered, in order that we may offer hearty prayers in common for ourselves, for the baptized person, and for all others in every place . . . Having ended the prayers, we salute one another with a holy kiss" (First Apology LXI.lxv).

Commentators have written much on "the holy kiss." We can be sure it does not teach promiscuous kissing. The kiss common in eastern lands was planted on the cheek, forehead, beard, or hands, not on the lips. Moreover, according to the *International Standard Bible Encyclopedia*, men as a rule only thus greeted men, and women, women ("Kiss," p. 1814). It was so ordered in the *Constitutions of the Holy Apostles*, "And let the deacon say to all, 'Salute one another with a holy kiss!' And let the clergy salute the bishop, the men of the laity salute the men, the women [salute] the women" (VIII.xi).

In our day the equivalent of this biblical greeting would be a hearty handshake. Linguists point out two basic types of acceptable translations for the concept of "kiss." The first is termed *formal* equivalence. The form of the source text is meticulously reproduced in the reader's language. A holy kiss remains a holy kiss.

The second kind of translation is called *dynamic* equivalence, in which the meaning of the original text is so transferred into the reader's language that the response of the reader is basically the same as that of the original readers. In our times and culture a holy kiss becomes a warm handshake.

Following are some paraphrases of Paul's and Peter's commands based on the dynamic equivalence translation:

"Salute one another with a hearty handshake" (Romans 16:16).
"Greet one another with a hearty handshake" (I Corinthians 16:20).
"Greet one another with a handshake all around" (I Peter 5:14).
"Greet each other with a warm handshake" (II Corinthians 13:12).
"Greet all the brethren with a warm handshake" (I Thessalonians 5:26).

PURPOSE OF THE GREETING

Such warm greetings among believers would serve to promote peace, unity and love in the church. It is hard to shake hands with a person unless you are on good terms with him. Once when D. L. Moody was giving a lecture to a group of ministers, a young pastor blurted out a remark which, though frank, was not rude. Moody snapped an answer back, then continued his lecture. Moody's response was not savagely uttered but was sharp enough so that the young man cringed at the rebuke. All in the chapel felt for him but the uncomfortable atmosphere gradually dissipated.

As Moody reached the close of his lecture, he paused, then said, "Friends, I want to confess before you all that I made a great mistake at the beginning of this meeting. I answered my young brother down there foolishly. I ask God to forgive me. And I ask him to forgive me."

And before anyone realized what was happening, the world's best-known evangelist stepped down from the platform, hurried over to the unknown youth and shook his hand. Had not Moody first made peace through his apology, it would have been difficult to shake hands.

The Corinthian church had been anything but peaceful. Carnality had caused contentions so that various cliques feuded over preachers, championing favorites and downgrading others. Some bragged about their spiritual gifts. Other believers took fellow Christians to law before heathen courts. Still others gorged themselves with the abundance of food they brought to the love feast preceding communion, while people sat nearby with hardly any food.

Only members of their own clique were greeted genuinely, while others were given a halfhearted nod or completely ignored. No wonder Paul ended both Corinthians epistles with a command to greet each other warmly. This would certainly help unfriendly factions to "tarry one for another" when they came to the love feast, or to clear the air of whatever was causing the friction (I Corinthians 11:33).

The command at the close of II Corinthians is preceded by a strong plea for peace. "Finally, brethren, farewell. Be perfect, be of good comfort, be of one mind, live in peace; and the God of love and peace shall be with you." Then he commands, "Greet one another with an holy kiss" (II Corinthians 13:11,12). So close is the plea for peace to the command to greet that another version translates this verse, "Greet one another with the kiss of peace."

Since this command would embrace every one of the brethren, not just those in one's own particular group, some sort of unity would have to be established before the kiss could mean much. If disputes were not first settled, any demonstration of affection would be awkward and insincere, like a Judas' kiss.

Wouldn't Euodias and Syntyche, the two ladies of Philippi at odds with each other, find it rather embarrassing to exchange a kiss of peace when peace did not exist? Wouldn't the thought of having to greet any estranged fellow believer in this warm way help to hasten honest attempts at reconciliation?

The communion at the Lord's Supper and the union expressed by the holy kiss were closely related. How could one take communion with any saint whom he could not in all sincerity warmly embrace in real Christian union? In fact, instructions for the Lord's Supper in the *Constitutions of the Holy Apostles* of about the third century said, "Let that deacon . . . say to the people, 'Let no one have any dispute with another; let no one come in hypocrisy.' Then let the men give the men, and the women give the women, the Lord's kiss" (II.vii).

A second purpose of the holy kiss was to promote love. A columnist received a letter from a girl who painted a vivid portrait of her father weeping uncontrollably beside his brother's casket and finally having to be physically removed from the cemetery.

The daughter gave the real reason for his distraught attitude as guilt more than grief, because for many years he had kept saying he had neither the time nor the money to see his brother. She added, "Now when it's too late he found both the time and the money. I have never seen anyone so broken up as my father." Then the daughter urged people to see loved ones now before it's too late.

Paul urges Christian brothers and sisters not only to attend the Lord's house where they will see their Christian family members, but also to greet them warmly and heartily.

As a stranger, have you ever attended a church where the atmosphere was cold and forbidding? No one greeted you at the door, "Good morning, I'm so glad to see you." After the service everyone filed out formally and politely, barely speaking to one another, or just barely nodding or grunting in your direction. A vigorous, genuine handshake would have dispelled the refrigerator climate, broken down barriers, fostered fellowship and encouraged a return visit.

A little boy was playing on a mountain near his home where the echo brought back his every statement. Running home one day he told his mother there was a boy out there who mocked and mimicked him and even threatened to fight him. The wise mother smiled, "Run out again and shout, I love you, and see what answer comes."

So the boy ran out and shouted, "I love you." And the echo replied, "I love you."

In many churches, members greet others with a quick word or unenthusiastic nod, which in turn draws an equally insipid and unanimated reply. As John enters, he sees Tom whom he may not especially care for. "Morning, Tom," he mumbles. Tom echoes the same subzero greeting. Had John given Tom a warm word and a hearty handshake to back it up, Tom would doubtless have responded in kind. Both would have felt better, perhaps even sensing a surge of love within for each other. Peter

143

doesn't misname this greeting when he calls it "the kiss of love," for it shows and seals the affection with which members of the same spiritual household should cherish each other.

THE POWER OF THE GREETING

Some of the value of this greeting comes from the power of touch. A small child falls and bruises her knee. Running home, she is enfolded in her mother's arms, who says, "Come, we'll wash it off." The healing began, not with the first aid cream, but with the comfort of Mother's touch.

The adult skin has over a million pain receptors scattered everywhere throughout the body. The tongue and the fingertips are the most sensitive, being able to detect two closely-spaced prongs of a hairpin, whereas the rest of the body feels them as a single piece.

Psychological tests reveal that infants who are not touched lovingly suffer emotional deprivation as adults. A baby should be kissed, hugged, held and touched every day.

But the basic need to be touched and comforted continues through life. One counselor advises holding your child on your lap if you're watching TV unless he's bigger than you are, ruffling your son's hair or patting his arm as you pass by, or giving him a kiss goodnight. Perhaps the entire family needs to be more physically affectionate. Older folks need to be touched, also, as well as the ill. Experiments show that people in deep comas often show improved heart rates when their hands are held by doctors or nurses.

A mother suddenly lost her baby in death. Hearing the tragic news, a friend hurried over and held the sorrowing mother's hand. No words were spoken. The mother said later, "Oh, the comfort of her touch."

For many, touching is taboo, for it represents an invasion of privacy. William Barclay in his book, *A Spiritual Autobiography,* confesses his disdain of baring his soul. Though gregarious, he likes to keep his distance. He suggests some connection between his desire for reticence and his general dislike of being touched.

For most of us, however, touching is a therapeutic activity. Though we can communicate by a glance or a word, the more intimate way is by the hand. Visitors in Cairo have noted how often males walk down the street holding hands. Touch says, "I really care."

The defensive squad of Ohio State's 1975 football team who were undefeated until the Rose Bowl held hands in every huddle between plays. The Rose Bowl TV announcer commented that this practice showed the togetherness of the team.

Though homosexuality is certainly more open today, no one should conclude that a sign of affection for someone of the same sex implies homosexuality. Sometimes, otherwise instructive articles on singleness have caused unnecessary worries by advising readers to steer clear of close same-sex relationships. Many today draw back from the warm hug, the squeeze of a hand, the pat on the head, or the cry on the shoulder.

One college graduate told his counselor of a time in his undergraduate days when he was very lonely. Going to the barbershop, the student was startled by the warm sensation that came over him when the barber's hand touched his neck. He wondered if he had sinful inclinations until it dawned on him that he had not experienced human touch for weeks.

Northern European and North American societies are

You Don't Have to Go It Alone

more reserved about touching. Russian diplomats greet each other with a warm type of bear hug; Latin cultures also encourage demonstrative affection. Often in our country an athlete who scores a goal or makes an outstanding play will be surrounded and hugged by his joyous, congratulatory teammates. Recently North American church circles have witnessed a noticeable increase of use of the warm hug and gentle kiss as a greeting.

Time and time again Jesus touched people—the leper, the blind, the deaf. He let John rest his head on His bosom at the Last Supper. He let a woman touch the hem of His garment. He let a woman of the city kiss and wipe His feet with her hair.

Gospel songwriters have caught up this thought with compositions like, "The Touch of His Hand on Mine," "Precious Lord, Take My Hand," and the more recently popular "He Touched Me."

A blow of the hand can be psychologically devastating but, conversely, the use of the hand to shake hands or to put around the shoulder, or to press an arm in encouragement, all speak of love and warmth. Touching is a tangible way of reaching out.

If the divine Son of God touched humanity, then should not redeemed men and women likewise reach out and touch someone?

12
Loving One Another

When a preacher announced his subject, "The Eleventh Commandment," some thought him dangerously innovative to attempt a postscript to the time-honored, all-inclusive Decalogue. Then he read his text: "A new commandment I give unto you, That ye love one another; as I have loved you, that ye also love one another. By this shall all men know that ye are my disciples, if ye have love one to another" (John 13:34,35).

Helen Steiner Rice wrote:

> The greatest need
>   in the world today is love . . .
> More love for each other
>   and more love for God above![17]

THE MANDATE TO LOVE

Love is commanded. Three times in the above text we

are enjoined to love one another. Contrary to romantically regarding love as some irrational and uncontrollable urge which suddenly looms from nowhere to irresistably topple an unsuspecting victim head over heels, biblical love involves the whole person, including intellect and will as well as emotions.

The promise "to love till death do us part" in the marriage ceremony demands subsequent, repeated acts of the will in the marriage situation. Each partner will make a deliberate effort to discover new reasons for admiring the other. By a conscious act of volition each must determine, "I *will* put her first; I *will* be kind to him; I *will* be patient."

Similarly, because Jesus Christ has mandated that His followers love each other, we are not merely to have pleasant feelings toward fellow believers if the mood strikes us, but we are to make strong effort to suffer long, be kind, envy not, be selfless, be even-tempered, think kindly of others and believe and hope for the best from them. Love is not to be considered a fluttering feeling, but is to be pursued with mind and will.

Though called "a new commandment," the injunction to love is really an old commandment, for it was part of the Mosaic law (Leviticus 19:18). Many Old Testament laws were based on neighborly love, such as returning a neighbor's lost animal or garment, or building protection around a roof to keep others from falling off (Deuteronomy 22:1-5,8).

John calls love no new commandment but "an old commandment which ye had from the beginning" (I John 2:7; 3:11; II John 5). In reality, the commandment went back to Old Testament time. It is a repeated commandment, for no command recurs as frequently as the exhortation to love one another.

Paul spoke of loving without hypocrisy (Romans 12:9). He gave us the famous love chapter (I Corinthians 13). He prayed for greater love in the hearts of the Philippians (Philippians 1:9). He was thankful for the love of the Colossians to all the saints and for the abounding love of the Thessalonians (Colossians 1:4; I Thessalonians 1:3).

The writer of Hebrews desired *brotherly love* to continue (Hebrews 13:1). The phrase, *brotherly love*, translated more accurately *love of brethren*, gives us our English *Philadelphia*, the type of love which is "scarcely found except in Christian writings," according to the *Pulpit Commentary*.

Not forgetting his Master's words, Peter calls for fervent, unfeigned love of the brotherhood (I Peter 1:22; 2:17; 4:8). John repeated the Savior's emphasis on love (I John 3:11-18; 4:7,8,11,12,16,20,21).

Love is also the most comprehensive of commandments. In the whole gamut of "one another" duties of the New Testament, all others can be subsumed under some aspect of love. Caring, burden-bearing, forgiving, preferring, honoring, receiving, admonishing, serving, forbearing, being kind, submitting, practicing hospitality—all can be classified under love one to another.

Paul shows how love is the fulfillment of the law. When you love your neighbor you do not break up his marriage by committing adultery with his wife, nor do you violate your neighbor's property by stealing it, nor defame your neighbor's reputation by false witness. Since love works no ill toward one's neighbor, love is the fulfilling of the law (Romans 13:8-10). John wrote, "And this is love, that we walk after his commandments" (II John 6). Thus, the eleventh commandment is really a summation of the previous ten.

You Don't Have to Go It Alone

Yet, Jesus said He was giving a new commandment. If love goes back to Old Testament times, why does Jesus say, "A new commandment I give unto you"? It is the linking of the command with Jesus Christ that is new. We are to love one another as Jesus Christ loved us. The command to love is old, but the command to love as Jesus loved is new.

THE MODEL OF LOVE

A Sunday school teacher was reviewing a lesson his class was supposed to know. "What made Jesus come into the world?" No one answered. Irritated, he repeated the question, "Why did Jesus come?" Still no answer. Finally, he exploded: "Love! Love!" Marching around the room, he roared out, "Love!" as he hit each child on the head with a ruler.

Jesus didn't shout love; rather, He showed it. He is the model of love. The order to love becomes a new commandment because of a new standard—Jesus' love. Just as He loved us, so should we love each other. How did Jesus express His love to us? Here are some characteristics found in the immediate context.

A stooping love. John 13 begins with Jesus stooping to wash the disciples' feet. This pictures His condescension from heaven to earth. He didn't grasp after self glory. He who was God became man. He who was Master became servant. He who was Somebody became a nobody, one of no reputation. He who was Life died the ignominious death reserved for criminals, aliens, and slaves. To display His love, we too must be willing to leave our ivory palaces and minister in a world of woe to the least, the last, the lowly and the lost.

A serving love. Immediately following the foot washing

150

Jesus said, "If I then . . . have washed your feet; ye also ought to wash one another's feet" (John 13:14). He did not come to be ministered unto, but to minister. What a servant He was: traveling, teaching, doing good, working miracles, healing the sick, raising the dead, comforting the bereaved. Reflecting His love means ministering to one another's needs.

A suffering love. A better wording would be "long-suffering love." A wall plaque bore this prayer, "Lord, I shall be very busy today. I may forget Thee, but do not Thou forget me." Seemingly flippant at first, this petition really says, "Lord, my love may waver, but thank You that Your love is constant to the end." John 13 begins, Jesus ". . . loved them unto the end" (verse 1).

Though foreseeing Peter's failure, Jesus treated him kindly. Similarly, despite His full knowledge of our foibles and failures, He loves us unconditionally.

Soon after issuing this new commandment to love, Jesus was severely mistreated. Yet, when reviled, He reviled not. On the cross He prayed for His tormentors, "Father, forgive them, for they know not what they do." His forbearing love was extended to the repentant thief who a few minutes before had been railing at Him. We are specifically told to follow such an example (I Peter 2:21,22).

A sacrificial love. Toward the end of his life, observing the crumbling of civilization with all of its viciousness and suffering, the well-known Harvard sociologist Pitirim Sorokin insisted that mankind needed a new science which he called *amitology*, after the Latin verb which means *to love*. Unless love was taught and caught, he affirmed repeatedly, civilization was doomed.

At the Last Supper in the upper room, Jesus repeated the commandment, ". . . That ye love one another, as I

151

You Don't Have to Go It Alone

have loved you." Then He added, "Greater love hath no man than this, that a man lay down his life for his friends" (John 15:12,13).

Probably the best known verse in the Bible, John 3:16, tells of Christ giving His life that we might have eternal life. But how many know the other John 3:16—I John 3:16? This verse challenges us to make the same sacrifice: "Because he laid down his life for us . . . we ought to lay down our lives for the brethren."

Because most of us will never be called on to die for fellow believers, John tells us in the next verse that we ought to make lesser sacrifices for the brethren. "But whoso hath this world's good, and seeth his brother have need, and shutteth up his bowels of compassion from him, how dwelleth the love of God in him?" (I John 3:17).

At a National Prayer Breakfast in Washington, Congressman Albert Quie related the tale of a busy commuter, Mr. Jones, hurrying through the station to catch his train to work, when he noticed a crippled lad selling apples. Suddenly another hurrying man accidentally knocked over the apple stand, scattering apples in every direction. The man paused momentarily, uttered a meaningless apology, then hurried so as not to miss his train.

Mr. Jones stopped for a moment, then resumed his hurrying. About to board the departing train, he had second thoughts. He went back to help the crippled boy. He noticed that the boy was also blind for he was desperately reaching in all directions for the apples.

Mr. Jones picked up every apple, polished each one with his clean handkerchief, re-erected the toppled stand and put the apples back in place.

As Mr. Jones was about to leave to catch the next train, the blind, crippled boy frantically grabbed his coat asking, "Say, Mister, are you Jesus?"

"No," said Mr. Jones, "but I want to be like Him."

THE MONOGRAM OF LOVE

Many companies have trademarks. Teams have uniforms. Officers wear badges. Hospital employees have marks of identification. Different symbols have been used to distinguish Christians, such as a cross or the fish. Nothing is wrong with these insignia of faith, but Jesus gave a label, not just for one locality or century, but for all places in all times. Here is the monogram:

> *By this shall all men know*
> *that ye are my disciples,*
> *if ye have love one to another.*

The badge of discipleship is not orthodoxy, oratory, scintillating knowledge of the Bible, faith or possession of any particular gift, but *love for one another.*

The emphasis is on love for the brethren, but the command does not annul the need for loving the unsaved. Through creation, all men are made in God's image and so must be treated humanely. Love must be extended to any person in need, in accordance with the Good Samaritan story. But if it is so important to love all men, how much more vital to love those with whom we are linked by special bonds. "Let us do good unto all men, especially unto them who are of the household of faith" (Galatians 6:10).

Jesus refers to something visible, therefore observable. This recognizable trademark of love among the brethren signifies the wearer as a true disciple of Christ. Observable love is a badge of the genuineness of the Christian faith. Though Christians may judge each other by their adherence to creed, the outside world, although uninterested in correct doctrine, does take note of kind devotion among professed followers of Christ.

A non-professing Christian visiting the Holy Land toured the various sites of Jesus' life—Bethlehem, Nazareth, Galilee, Gethsemane and the Mount of Olives—and had some cloud of doubt flit across his mind. Was the Christian faith historically accurate? Did Jesus ever visit the earth? Then, recalling acts of love in the lives of believers back home, he was again convinced of the reality of Christianity. The practice of love will arrest an unbelieving world and convince it of the truth of the "faith." If the injunction to love is obeyed the insignia of love will be displayed.

The failure of Christians to love each other doesn't prove they are not genuine believers, but it does give the outside world the perfect right to wonder whether or not they are real Christians. Just as a bona fide hospital worker may be stopped by a security officer because he's not displaying his official badge, so the world may make a wrong judgment about a believer who is not showing brotherly love. If the badge of love is missing, we cannot expect the non-Christian to recognize we are Christians or to decide that Christianity is for real.

The insignia of love doesn't mean that Christians cannot disagree with each other, but it does imply that they disagree agreeably, even lovingly. Christians have not always presented a pretty picture to the world. Too often the non-Christian has been turned off because he has failed to see the beauty of love in the professing Christian. A non-Christian photographer had hit an impasse in his attempt to get two lady faculty members at a Bible college together for a picture. When he discovered that his problem stemmed from their mutual dislike, he was heard to mingle an oath with these words, "If this is Christianity, I want nothing to do with it."

Dr. Francis Schaeffer says, "I have observed one thing among true Christians in their differences in many countries: What divides and severs true Christian groups and Christians—what leaves a bitterness that can last for 20, 30, or 40 years (or for 50 or 60 years in a son's memory)—is not the issue of doctrine or belief which caused the difference in the first place. Invariably it is lack of love—and the bitter things that are said by true Christians in the midst of differences.

"These stick in the mind like glue . . . It is these things—these unloving attitudes and words—that cause the stench that the world can smell in the church of Jesus Christ among those who are really true Christians . . . The world looks, shrugs its shoulders and turns away . . . It has not seen even the beginning of what Jesus indicates is the final apologetic—observable oneness among true Christians who are truly brothers in Christ. Our sharp tongues, the lack of love between us—not necessary statements of differences that may exist between true Christians—these are what properly trouble the world."[18]

When one Christian dragged another Christian before the pagan courts in Corinth the unbelieving judges must have laughed. Paul called such a practice a shame, urging instead love that would suffer financial reverse rather than go to a heathen court which would not see any observable love. These unsaved judges would have the right to make the horrible judgment that Christianity was not genuine.

What good is doctrinal truth if those who hold to it are ugly! This is why Bertrand Russell sighed, "The trouble with Christ was that He had disciples." And Mark Twain put it, "If Christ were here now, there is one thing He would not be—a Christian."

By all means we must learn apologetics so we are prepared to give an answer to every man that asks the reason for the hope that is within us. But the proper answer, if contradicted by lack of love displayed among believers, will become the diversion that will lead the seeker astray.

In the article, "Biblical Marks of a Succeeding Church," Dr. Bruce Shelly said, "Unfortunately, many churches today fail to see additions to their numbers because they have no real fellowship. When a family breaks into an open feud, a guest feels embarrassed. No one wants to be around a tension-filled household. The reason some churches do not grow is simple: they are not pleasant places to be around. But show me a congregation where people love each other, enjoy hours spent together, care for each other and serve members in need, and I will show you a growing, succeeding church. There is magnetism in genuine Christian fellowship."[19]

Brother-love has an evangelistic impact. A gracious disposition, charitable words, and kind deeds will convince observers of the truth of the faith. What love was exhibited in the apostolic church at Jerusalem, as the well-to-do shared their possessions with the needy! It was no wonder that through this observable love people were saved and added to the church daily (Acts 2:44-47). No wonder the apostles were able to preach the resurrection of Christ with "great power" (Acts 4:32,33).

When the first religious friction broke out between the Hellenist and Hebraic elements in the Jerusalem church, the gracious love exercised in solving the conflict made its impact on the unsaved community. "And the word of God increased; and the number of the disciples multiplied in Jerusalem greatly; and a great company of the priests were obedient to the faith'' (Acts 6:7).

When the Gentiles at Antioch and in Greece sent financial assistance to the poor Jews at Jerusalem, this incident made a dramatic impact on the unsaved world. Missionary work was enhanced. Tertullian wrote, ''But it is mainly the deeds of a love so noble that lead many to put a brand upon us. 'See,' they say, 'how they love one another.' For they themselves will rather put to death'' (Apology XXXIX).

This type of outreach has been termed *fellowship* evangelism in distinction to *mass* evangelism (Peter preaching at Pentecost) and *personal* evangelism (Philip witnessing to the Ethiopian eunuch).

Evangelical Missions Information Service, based on interviews and visits to mainland China in 1974, reports that the fervent, faithful love Chinese believers have for each other causes many a non-Christian neighbor to inquire into the nature of their faith. Observance of this love makes them desire Jesus for themselves.

Says an unknown poet:

> The church that hopes to win the lost
> Must pay the one unchanging cost;
> She must compel the world to see
> In her the Christ of Calvary.

During the Italian occupation of Ethiopia in the days of Mussolini, the believers suffered considerable persecution. In his book, *Fire on the Mountains,* Raymond Davis tells of the love demonstrated by believers for each other during the period of affliction, which in turn made a major impression on unbelievers. For example, no provision was made to feed the prisoners in jail. This was the responsibility of relatives and friends. Believers in the prisons were well cared for by friends and family. In fact, so much food was brought them by fellow believers and church groups that enough remained to feed the unbelieving prisoners also.

This observable love, vibrant though nonverbal, brought many to seek the Lord. Such love was previously unheard of. As a result the word spread far and wide. Non-believers sought out believers to learn more about the Christian faith. When prisoners who had come to know Christ while in jail were released, they went back home and attended the nearest church.

Doesn't the song say, "And they'll know we are Christians by our love"?

Notes

1. Excerpt from *In the Presence of Mine Enemies* by Howard and Phyllis Rutledge with Mel and Lyla White. Copyright © 1973 by Fleming H. Revell Company. Used with permission.

2. John Broadus, *Commentary on Matthew* (American Baptist Publication Society, 1886), p. 218.

3. From poem, "Opposites" (New York: Harcourt Brace Jovanovich, Inc.). Reprinted with permission from the April 1975 *Reader's Digest.*

4. Howard A. Snyder, *The Problem of Wine Skins* (Downers Grove, IL: InterVarsity Press, 1976), pp. 139-40. Used with permission.

5. "On Bearing One Another's Burdens," by editorial staff, *Christianity Today* (March 25, 1975), p. 651. Used with permission.

6. Poem, "The World Would Be A Nicer Place If We Traveled At A Slower Pace," by Helen Steiner Rice, Fleming H. Revell Company. Used with permission.

7. "The Confession of Sin," *Christian Heritage* (April, 1974), p. 9.

8. William Barclay, *Letters to the Romans* (Glasgow, Scotland: Westminster Press, 1962), p. 199.

9. Hudson Armerding, *Leadership* (Wheaton, IL: Tyndale House, 1979), p. 167. Used with permission.

10. John A. Broadus, *Commentary on the Gospel of Matthew* (Philadelphia: American Baptist Publication Society, 1886), p. 391.

11. Michael R. Tucker, *The Church That Dared To Change* (Wheaton, IL: Tyndale House, 1975), p. 94. Used with permission.

12. James R. Adair, *M. R. DeHaan, the Man and His Ministry* (Grand Rapids, MI: Zondervan Publishing House, 1969), p. 129. Used with permission.

13. Leslie B. Flynn, *19 Gifts of the Spirit* (Wheaton, IL: Victor Books, 1974), p. 204.

14. Excerpt from *In the Presence of Mine Enemies* by Howard and Phyllis Rutledge with Mel and Lyla White. Copyright © 1973 by Fleming H. Revell Company. Used with permission.

15. T.H.L. Parker, *Portraits of Calvin* (SCM Press, Ltd.), p. 25.

16. *Prairie Overcomer*, (April, 1977), p. 203.

17. Poem by Helen Steiner Rice, Fleming H. Revell Company. Used with permission.

18. Francis A. Schaeffer, *The Mark of the Christian* (Downers Grove, IL: InterVarsity Press, 1979), pp. 22-23. Used with permission.

19. "Biblical Marks of a Succeeding Church," *United Evangelical Action* (Winter, 1974), p. 19.